M000086795

TREASURY OF CALLIGRAPHY

TREASURY OF CALLIGRAPHY

219 Great Examples, 1522–1840

EDITED BY

JAN TSCHICHOLD

DOVER PUBLICATIONS, INC., NEW YORK

Copyright © 1984 by Dover Publications, Inc.
All rights reserved under Pan American and International Copyright Conventions.

This Dover edition, first published in 1984, is a translation of the second edition, 1949, of the work *Schatzkammer der Schreibkunst: Meisterwerke der Kalligraphie aus vier Jahrhunderten auf zweihundert Tafeln*, originally published by the Verlag Birkhäuser, Basel. All the plates are included; the new English translation of the text, by Stanley Appelbaum, is virtually complete, omitting only a few details of the list of sources, as noted on page xi.

Manufactured in the United States of America
Dover Publications, Inc., 31 East 2nd Street, Mineola, N.Y. 11501

Library of Congress Cataloging in Publication Data

Schatzkammer der Schreibkunst. English.
Treasury of calligraphy.

Translation of: Schatzkammer der Schreibkunst. 2nd ed. Basel: Birkhäuser, 1949.
Bibliography: p.
Includes index.
1. Calligraphy. 2. Paleography. I. Tschichold, Jan, 1902-1974.
II. Title.
Z43.S3613 1984 745.6′1 84-10323
ISBN 0-486-24700-7

CONTENTS

INTRODUCTION

A world history of art of the last two millennia which would give calligraphy the rank of an art has yet to be written. Such a work would have to treat of three great script civilizations: first, that of the very ancient calligraphy of China, an ideographic script that is used far beyond the linguistic borders of China and, very much alive today, is considered the equal of painting as an art form. Next would come the realm of Arabic writing, and thirdly that of our Occidental calligraphy. The latter two script civilizations are derived from a common Semitic mother, the Phoenician phonetic alphabet, from which were developed not only the Greek and Roman letters (and thus our writing) but also the Arabic letters, those highly meritorious forms—some monumental, some cursive—that still enjoy constant use in large parts of the Near East.

Western calligraphy perished long ago. Its periods of glory were late antiquity and the European middle ages. Only a few connoisseurs still know what perfection was attained, after the scribes of late Greek times, by those of late Roman days and above all by the monks of medieval Christendom. Paleography, the science of old writing, is considered merely an auxiliary aid to historiography. Paleographers regard medieval scripts as nothing but historical documents, never as artistic expressions, and are concerned only with deciphering them. Therefore we still lack a continuous collection, chosen for artistic values alone, of the most beautiful writing of the middle ages between 800 and 1500. Such a collection could only be assembled by a wearisome and painful search through countless archives and manuscript departments of libraries, and unfortunately can scarcely be expected nowadays. Surely the book and correspondence hands between 1000 and 1450 would especially repay such an effort. An art history of the hands of this period would provide us with a criterion of script beauty and many stimuli for a new evolution. Not driven by that haste which is one of the chief evils of our times, the scribes of the medieval monasteries produced numerous examples—fortunately still preserved—of splendid artistic writing that is in no way inferior to the Chinese and Arabo-Persian masterpieces.

When printing was invented and education was no longer a privilege of the clergy, medieval calligraphy was doomed. The book, up to then an object of monastic scribal industry, became the chief article produced by the secular printer. Calligraphy is associated with books only to the extent that it provided the printer with the typefaces that are still his most important means of expression today. And even if no one can design good typefaces without being thoroughly versed in calligraphy, nevertheless since Gutenberg's invention the art of typography has had to follow the special laws of printing and go its own way.

The heirs to medieval calligraphy were the chancery clerks of princely courts and those teachers who taught reading, writing and arithmetic to anyone desirous of learning. Writing became a middle-class ability; nearly everyone thenceforth could write a letter or draw up a bill.

In order to ease the burden of teaching and probably also to give others the opportunity to learn to write without a teacher, many writing masters published instructions with examples of currently used hands. Between 1500 and 1800 some eight hundred such copybooks appeared. They have become very rare and well-guarded treasures in libraries. The former State Library for Fine and Applied Art in Berlin owned over four hundred; another extensive collection was that of the library of the financial organization of German bookdealers in Leipzig. A large collection of chiefly English copybooks is owned by Mr. Ambrose Heal of Beaconsfield, the author of the careful bibliography *The English Writing-Masters and Their Copy-Books*. In Switzerland the library of the Gewerbemuseum in Basel, which acquired a sizable collection of old copybooks during the administration of Hermann Kienzle, is the outstanding one.

The last-named collection, my own and a few others provided the sources of the two hundred plates in the present volume. They constitute a survey covering more than three hundred years, going beyond the decline of Western calligraphy. The selection was made especially with the calligrapher in mind; it is meant to provide him with the historic examples he constantly needs in his work. We have not included hands that were too much of a current fad or have become incomprehensible today. The sequence is generally chronological by date of publication, not generic by style of writing. As a rule we have reproduced only a single original page on one of our pages, so that the examples do not fight one another; only the Italian and Spanish examples at the beginning are an exception. In addition, facing pages of this volume are almost always from the same source.

Italians, Spaniards and Germans begin the series of copybooks in the first half of the sixteenth century. Their examples are very carefully cut in wood, some in relief (black on white) and some in intaglio (white on black) following the grain—that is, in the same technique as the book illustrations of the period. Ludovico Vicentino's beautiful volume (Plate 1) was not the first, but, alongside Giambattista Palatino's often reprinted little book, one of the most widely distributed printed copybooks of the time.

Cursive was the script of the Italian and Spanish south, even if Gerardus Mercator in Amsterdam also helped disseminate it in a beautiful volume (plates 2 and 3). The simple and clear forms of its Italian derivative, *cancellaresca*, still remain unsurpassable models for a good commercial hand. Of lapidary nobility are the cursive examples of the Spaniard Francisco Lucas (Plates 17–19), while those of the Italian Vespasiano Amphiareo (Plates 20 and 21) are more graceful. Alongside cursive, common Spanish styles were the elegant *redondilla* (Plates 14 and 15) and, for special purposes, the *redonda*, a holdover from the Gothic period, which Juan de Yciar preserved in a magnificent, cleverly ornamental alphabet (Plates 10–13). Vespasiano (Plates 22 and 23) and Yciar (Plate 9) also acquaint us with derivatives of cursive as used by contemporary merchants.

In the north, the characteristic commercial scripts were Fraktur, Kanzlei and Kurrent. *Fraktur* ("broken script"; as in Plate 43), which had been developed by Leonard Wagner in Augsburg about 1507, was a titling script that from 1525 was also used as a body type. *Kanzlei* ("chancery"; as in Plate 28) was less stiff and thus written more rapidly. *Kurrent* ("cursive"; as in Plate 72), the easiest to learn and most flowing form of German writing, finally led to that ugly German cursive that was generally taught until about 1910.

As early as 1519 Johann Neudörffer in Nuremberg had published models of German hands. We reproduce a few leaves from his 1538 publication *Anweysung einer gemeinen hanndschrift*, which he himself engraved, without reversing, on copper plates. The final pages, produced by transfer and thus seldom cleanly printed, were hand-decorated by the master with calligraphic ornaments and gold lines (Plates 24–33). Nevertheless his laborious printing method did not become standard practice. The woodcut held its own for many decades more, even though the hollowing out of the wood around the slender letters was an extremely difficult task that could be entrusted only to experienced woodblock cutters who understood lettering.

A follower of all the above-named masters was the Swiss Urban Wyss, who translated their models in his own good-looking books with his own personal sense of form (Plates 34–39). A mine of variations on both northern "broken" scripts and southern cursive scripts is the 1549 Cologne *Schatzkamer* (Treasury) of Caspar Neff, which has lent its title to the present book. Gothic styles are still in evidence in the models of the Nuremberg master Wolffgang Fugger (Plates 54 and 55) and in the later sheets by Urban Wyss (Plates 56 and 57), reminiscent of Dürer's title pages, while in Italy the

Renaissance has already unfurled, giving rise to the noble pages of men like Giovanni Cresci (Plates 58–64). Two English examples (Plates 65 and 66) betray the influence of Italian models; a third (Plate 67) is based directly on the late Gothic commercial hand that developed into bâtarde in France.

The pages by Johann Leupolt of Markörlbach (Plates 68–73) are reproduced from a manuscript "art book," not a printed one. They show the hands as they were actually written. The scripts of all printed copybooks had to suffer at least slight alterations, due partially to the laborious technical preparation and partially to a lack of understanding and to willfulness on the part of the woodblock cutters and copperplate engravers.

Hitherto unpublished, like the last-named samples, are also the impressive engravings from the copybook of Benignus Morellus, completely unknown up to now (Plates 74–79). They are characterized by a wise limitation to essentials, avoiding the curlicues that play an often overpowering role in almost all subsequent copybooks. At the same time they are among the first calligraphic models engraved on copper. This process begins to supplant woodcuts toward the end of the sixteenth century. Instead of laboriously hollowing out the areas around the letters, artists dug the letters into the metal plate. This was not always done with such enormous skill and perfect understanding as in the works of the great Dutchman Jan van den Velde (Plates 80–95), who was not only an unusually well-versed calligrapher, but also found in Frysius (see Plate 80) a master of the engraving art who did justice to every subtlety of his writing. While his writing was almost certainly not "beautified" by the engraver, the artistic ornaments could hardly have been drawn quite so perfectly on paper as they appear in the engraving. Nevertheless the original scripts probably did not differ significantly from the engravings. The amazing energy and harmony of all his letters is sufficient proof that Jan van den Velde possessed an unusually sure hand that could master even the most difficult tasks.

Charmingly naïve, almost like a schoolboy's work, in contrast to these splendid cosmopolitan pages, are the somewhat clumsy models of the Swiss Caspar Rütlinger (Plates 96–99), which are based on various earlier masters, including Vespasiano. By comparison, the well-engraved, noble scripts of the Italian Francesco Pericciolì produce a sure and light effect, while the ornamental tangles in the margins of his pages are boring (Plates 100–103).

On one of the pages by the Lyons master François Desmoulins (Plate 105), the sparingly used and dramatic ornaments make a desirable and fully convincing contribution. On other pages (Plates 107 and 109–111) Desmoulins offers probably the most graceful applications of that calligraphic playfulness which ambitiously attempted to draw animals and people "in one stroke." Like Rütlinger's booklet, Desmoulins' rare work is also an attractive product of the efforts of a rural minor master.

Louis Barbedor (Plates 112–116) can be considered as the best French calligrapher of the seventeenth century. No less perfect in form than his letters are his few but boldly placed ornaments, the beauty of which almost transforms Barbedor's pages into pure pictures. His significant power of form is already evident in the constant variation of his signatures, each of which is an individual work of art. The larger scripts (e.g. Plate 116), as well as the ornaments, were written "with a free hand," that is, with elbow raised off the table and the entire arm set in movement. Many ornamented smaller letters (Plate 117) were also so written.

The next pages (Plates 118–121) are the work of the great Spaniard Joseph de Casanova, who did his own engraving because he did not credit the professional engravers with the necessary feeling for the fine details of his scripts. Here we find ornaments that go back to Moorish styles, like those in early Italian copybooks. They have a wild and impetuous look next to the courtly and smooth flourishes of Senault (Plates 124 ff.), who was probably a pupil of Barbedor or at any rate followed completely in his footsteps.

Two English examples by Charles Snell (Plates 128 and 129) lead into the eighteenth century, which we open with the Spaniard Aznar de Polanco (Plates 130–135). Just as fifteenth- and sixteenth-century calligraphers attempted to establish geometrically the proportions of ancient Roman monumental inscriptions, now there began a movement to examine constructionally, and to canonize, even the light, dynamic forms of cursive. As long as written forms were used as the basis of such efforts, this preference for the geometrical construction of letters still did no harm; it was the erroneous conception that one could construct scripts with compass and ruler without knowing how to write that led in the late nineteenth century and then once more in the recent past to a degeneration in letter forms.

The models of the Basel calligraphers J. J. Spreng (Plates 136 and 137) and Christoph Brunner (Plates 140–143) and those of Adolph Zunner of Nuremberg (Plates 138 and 139) show us the Rococo variations on German Kurrent and cursive in the German-speaking lands. Alongside the cosmopolitan cursives of the Englishmen J. Bland (Plates 144–149) and George Bickham (Plates 150–157) the Basel models appear petty bourgeois and almost timid. The attempts to assimilate German Kurrent to cursives merely brought German handwriting closer to the taste of the times and began to destroy its legibility.

The English examples, on the other hand, display a smoothness that becomes nearly unbearable. This is largely a result of the copperplate technique, the sharpness of engraving and elegance of which tempted calligraphers more and more to write "like an engraving." Pleasure was taken in the use of a highly pointed pen, and the natural broad sweep of the older pen began to yield to the artificial, pressure-produced swelling of the pointed pen. Then England's supremacy in world trade helped disseminate the English pointed-pen script, also called *anglaise*, throughout the world as a norm for European writing. But the early examples of anglaise from the eighteenth century are not without charm and are still exemplary in their genre. It is only the late, more highly polished forms, first appearing in the middle of the nineteenth century, that constitute the actual decline.

With the pages by Bernhard Menzzer (Plates 158 and 159), Jean Braun (Plates 160–163) and J. J. Brunner (Plates 164 and 165) we return to the continent, which appears a little backward in these German, Alsatian and Swiss examples. An exception to this, however, is the beautiful French copybook by Paillasson (Plates 166–173), still written with a broad pen—although not totally devoid of artificial pressure—and combining elegance with artistic expression. Among the most pleasurable works of Swiss calligraphy is the volume by J. J. Roschi of Berne (Plates 174 and 175). He is already writing even German Kurrent with a pointed pen and artificial pressure; only the Fraktur headings (which of course cannot be written any other way) show a broad-pen ductus. We once again meet the forms of German Kurrent using broad pen (Plates 176–180) and a somewhat odd but not unattractive "German" version of cursive (Plate 181) before we come upon (Plates 182–185) the beginnings of that degenerate form of German handwriting that was still taught in the first decades of this century and is already half forgotten today. Even if German Kurrent has since dropped out of use as a commercial hand, nevertheless the calligrapher will be able to use its older forms occasionally, and connoisseurs will delight in its rich variations.

The scripts on the last plates of our book become yet more distant from the original written forms and are partially invented and constructed on the drawing board. The imagination of the calligraphers even leads them to absurdities (Plates 194 and 197). Lithography, a real pointed-pen technique, favored these design excesses in every way. Fifty years later the first signs of a renewal of writing were to appear.

After the introduction of the form-destroying sharp steel pen the use of the typewriter destroyed the last remains of earlier calligraphy in the entire realm of Western civilization. Since any attempt to undo this course of events seems foolhardy, we must resign ourselves to the elegiac realization that Western calligraphy as a common possession belongs to the past and today is still maintained by only a handful of artists. The few people who care about calligraphy or even about fine handwriting today—a small elite of not more than some twenty people in Europe and North America—lack a living groundwork, a general practice of good writing.

This book is not primarily a model book, but a collection of selected characteristic examples of fine hands from the last three centuries that are deserving of careful study.

If the beginning designer of scripts imitates his master's scripts he will probably always remain his pupil. Therefore he should return to the sources and exhaust them on his own. The learner can never do enough writing. Merely looking at good forms of handwriting is barely of any use. Only through active study can the learner comprehend the forms of writing. He should only begin to *design* scripts after he has really learned how to write. This is not learned in four weeks. It takes patience and perseverance. But scarcely any other activity creates so much harmony in a person's entire being, and so calligraphy can be recommended to everyone. The incipient master will discern that the scripts of the end of the eighteenth and first half of the nineteenth centuries are unprofitable degenerate phenomena, and that new health for calligraphy can be attained above all by a thorough study of the forms created between 1500 and 1700. I hope that this volume, the greater part of which was printed in troubled wartime, will contribute to this recovery.

SOURCES OF THE PLATES

TRANSLATOR'S NOTE: The titles are given exactly as on the original title pages. The plate numbers shown are those of Tschichold's anthology, not those of the original copybooks. Names of the owner-lenders of the originals, where supplied by Tschichold in the German-language edition, appear here inside parentheses. Omitted here, because of the difference in format between the German-language edition and Dover's, are Tschichold's statements relative to the size of the reproductions ("original size," "slightly reduced," etc.).

BARBEDOR. Les ecritures financiere, et italienne-bastarde dans leur naturel. Par Louis Barbedor. Paris, Pierre Drevet, n.d. [ca. 1647]. (Aarau, Kantonsbibliothek.) Plates 112–116.

BEAUCHESNE-BAILDON. A booke containing divers sortes of hands by J. de Beauchesne and John Baildon. London? 1571. From Lewis F. Day, *Penmanship*, London, Batsford, n.d. Plates 65–67.

BICKHAM. The Universal Penman. Engrav'd by George Bickham. London, 1743. Plates 150–157.

BLAND. Kurtze und gründliche Anweisung, nach der neuesten Art zierlich zu Schreiben, n.p., n.d. [J. Bland, London sculp.]. One plate bears the date 1739. Not listed by Heal. (Jan Tschichold, Basel.) Plates 144–149.

BRAUN. Vorweisung verschiedener Teutsch- u. Französischer Schriften. Verfertigt von J[ean]. B[raun]. in Mülhausen [1774]. (Gewerbemuseum Basel.) Plates 160–163.

BRUNNER, CHRISTOPH. Vorschrifft/Deutsch und Frantzösischer Lauff Cantzley und Fraktur Schrifften. Durch Christoph Brunner Burger in Basel [1729]. (Gewerbemuseum Basel.) Plates 140–143.

BRUNNER, JOHANN JACOB. Vorschrift Zu nützlicher Nachahmung und einer fleissigen Übung zu gutem vorgestellt und geschrieben durch Joh: Jacob Brunner älter von Basel. Bern 1766. (Gewerbemuseum Basel.) Plates 164 and 165.

CASANOVA. Primera parte del arte de escrivir todas formas de letras. Escrito, y tallado por el maestro Ioseph de Casanova. En Madrid. Año 1650. (Jan Tschichold, Basel.) Plates 118–121.

CRESCI. Il perfetto Scrittore. Di M. Gio. Francesco Cresci, Venetia 1569 [Rome 1570?]. (Gewerbemuseum Basel.) Plates 58–64.

DESMOULINS. Le Paranimphe de les ecriture ronde financiere & jtalienne . . . de Francois Desmoulins Escrivain Le tout faict & graué par luy mesme. 1625. A Lyon. (Zurich, Kunstgewerbemuseum.) Plates 104–111.

FUGGER. Ein nutzlich vnd wolgegrundt Formular, Manncherleij schöner schriefften. Nürnberg, 1553. Plates 54 and 55.

HEINRIGS. Le Maitre d'Ecriture des Commerçans . . . Der Kaufmännische Schreibemeister . . . von Johann Heinrigs. Crefeld, 1813. (Universitätsbibliothek Basel.) Plates 184 and 185.

HEINRIGS. Symbolische-Kalligraphische Kunstblätter von I. Heinrigs. Cöln, bei dem Verfasser. 1831. Two issues. (Paul Morf, Basel.) Plates 194 and 195.

HOCHREUTINER. Formular Allerhand vblischster vnnd gemeinester Schrifften . . . verfertiget durch Johann Hochreütiner. [St. Gallen] 1658. (B. Burstein, Lugano.) Plates 122 and 123.

LEUPOLT. Kurtze Ordnung vnd Furweissung Artlichs vnd zierlichs Schreibens, Daraus dann ein Jeder mit rechtem grunnd die zierlichen Handschriffte begreiffen vnd Jre Fundament ersehen mag. Durch Johann Leupolt von Markörlbach, mit sonderm vleiss geordnet im Jahr Christi so man zelt M.D.xcvj [1596]. Manuscript on parchment. (Gewerbemuseum Basel.) Plates 68–73.

LUCAS. Arte de Escrivir de Francisco Lucas. Madrid. 1608. (Imre Reiner, Ruvigliana-Lugano.) Plates 13 (right)–19 (the illustration on the left side of Plate 18 is from the 1580 edition).

MENZZER. Anleitung zur Schönschreibekunst . . . von Johann Friedrich Bernhard Menzzer. Darmstadt 1775. (Gewerbemuseum Basel.) Plates 158 and 159.

MERCATOR, GERARDUS. Literarum Latinarum, quas Italicas, cursoriasque vocant, scribendarum ratio. Excudebat Antuerpiae Ioannes Richard. 1540. Plates 2 and 3.

MIDOLLE. Spécimen des ecritures modernes . . . exécutées à la plume par Jean Midolle. Strasbourg, 1834–35. (Gewerbemuseum Basel.) Plates 196–198.

MIDOLLE. Traité Complet d'Ecritures en tous genres et d'ornements moyen-âge d'après le système méthodique de J. Midolle. Publié par Tribelhorn à St Gall [1840]. (Jan Tschichold, Basel.) Plate 199.

MORELLUS. Exemplaria latinis characterib[us] ac Italicis confecta. Benigno Morello Ciuitatis Imp[er]ialis Bisuntinae [Besançon] ciue autore et i[n]ue[n]tore. [1606]. Probably a unique copy. (L'Art Ancien S.A., Zurich, Gartenstrasse 24.) Plates 74–79.

NEFF. Ein köstliche Schatzkamer der schreibkunst vnd Cleinott der Cantzley vnnd ander schreiber. Durch M. Caspar Neffenn. Köln 1549. (Universitätsbibliothek Basel.) Plates 42–45.

NEFF. Thesaurarium artis scriptoriae et Cancellariae Scribarumque Clenodium. Caspare Nevio Coloniae Agrippinae Scriba authore. Köln 1549. (Universitätsbibliothek Basel.) Plates 46–53.

NEUDÖRFFER. Ein gute Ordnung, vnd kurtze vnterricht. Durch Johann Newdörffer. Nürnberg 1538. — Anweysung einer gemeinen hanndschrift. Nürnberg 1538. Bound together. (Gewerbemuseum Basel.) Plates 24–33.

PAILLASSON. L'Art d'Ecrire réduit à des démonstrations vraies et Faciles, Avec des Explications claires, pour Le Dictionnaire des Arts. par Paillasson Expert Ecrivain Juré. [Paris] 1760. (Jan Tschichold, Basel.) Plates 166–173.

PALATINO. Libro di Giambattista Palatino nel quale s'insegna a scrivere ogni sorte lettera. Roma 1554 [?1553]. (Gewerbemuseum Basel.) Plates 4–7.

PERICCIOLI. Il terzo libro delle cancellaresche corsive et altre maniere di caratteri . . . inventati da Francesco Periccioli, Scrittore in Siena. Intagliato, per Martino Vanbuiten in Napoli. 1619. (Jan Tschichold, Basel.) Plates 100–103.

PETRÉ. Untitled copybook. Petré in[vent]or fecit. A Paris N. Langlois rüe St. Jacques à la Victoire. n.d. [ca. 1670]. From a bound "Senault" collection. (Gewerbemuseum Basel.) Plates 126, 127 and 200.

POLANCO. Arte nuevo de escribir . . . del Mro Juan Claudio Aznar de Polanco. Madrid, 1719. (Imre Reiner, Ruvigliana-Lugano.) Plates 130–135.

ROSCHI. Vorschrift zum Nuzen der Bernerischen Jugend, verfertiget durch Johann Jakob Roschi, Schreibmeister an der Kunstschule in Bern. Gegraben durch Heinrich Brupbacher in Wädischwyl. 1789. Bern bey C.A. Jenni. (Jan Tschichold, Basel.) Plates 174 and 175.

RÜTLINGER. Calligraphia nova. Capitalium et reliquarum literarum ultra xxx specimina scribendi. Per Casparum Rutlingerum. Tiguri [Zurich] 1615. (Gewerbemuseum Basel.) Plates 96–99.

SENAULT. Nouveau Liure d'Escriture Ronde et bastarde. Escrit et gravé par L. Senault. Paris, n.d. [ca. 1670]. From a bound "Senault" volume. (Gerwerbemuseum Basel.) Plates 117, 124, 125.

SNELL. The Pen-Man's Treasury Open'd. By Charles Snell Writing Master At the Golden Pen in Foster Lane. London [1694]. From Ambrose Heal, *The English Writing-Masters.* Plate 128.

SNELL. The Standard Rules of the Round and Round Text Hands. Invented by Charles Snell. London [1714]. From Ambrose Heal, *The English Writing-Masters.* Plate 129.

SPRENG. Grund-Riss der Schreib-Kunst Darinnen

die richtige Führung der Feder . . . vorstellet Johann Jacob Spreng, als Schreibm[eiste]r in Basel [ca. 1709]. (Liestal, Kantonal-Bibliothek.) Plates 136 and 137.

STEPHANI. Muster-Blätter fur den Schreibunterricht in Volks-Schulen von D. Heinrich Stephani. Erlangen, 1815. (Gewerbemuseum Basel.) Plates 182 and 183.

STIRLING. Bellezas de la Caligrafia. Por R. Stirling. Barcelona [1830]. (Gewerbemuseum Basel.) Plates 186–193.

STYMMER. Ein Nüw Kunstrych Fundamentbüchle von Mancherley . . . Schrifften . . . geschriben durch den Jungen Christoff Stymmer von Schaffhusen. Zürich 1549. Plates 40 and 41.

TAGLIENTE. Lo presente libro Insegna La vera arte de lo Excellente scrivere. [Venice] 1531. (Gewerbemuseum Basel.) Plate 8.

VELDE. Spieghel der Schrijfkonste. Door Jan vanden Velde. Rotterdam 1605. (Gewerbemuseum Basel.) Plates 80–95.

VESPASIANO. Opera di frate Vespasiano Amphiareo . . . nellaquale si insegna a scrivere varie sorti di lettere. In Venetia 1564. (Gewerbemuseum Basel.) Plates 20–23.

VICENTINO. La operina di Ludovico Vicentino, da imparare di scrivere littera Cancellaresca. Rome [1522]. (Gewerbemuseum Basel.) Plate 1.

VORSCHRIFTEN, deutsch, französisch und lateinisch, in XIX Blättern. Winterthur, in der Steinerischen Buchhandlung, 1805. (Gewerbemuseum Basel.) Plates 176–181.

WYSS. Ein neuw Fundamentbuch Darin allerley Tütsche Geschriffte . . . Zürich 1562. From Jessen, *Meister der Schreibkunst* (published by Dover as *Masterpieces of Calligraphy*, 24100–9). Plates 56 and 57.

WYSS. Libellus valde doctus, elegans & utilis, multa & varia scribendarum literarum genera complectens. Zürich 1549. (Gewerbemuseum Basel.) Plates 34–39.

YCIAR. Arte subtilissima, por la qual se enseña a escrevir perfectamente . . . por Juan de yciar vizcayno. Caragoça, M.D.L. [1550]. From illustrations in *L'Art pour tous*, Paris, ca. 1870. Plates 9–13 (left).

ZUNNER. Kunstrichtige Schreib-Art. Von Adolph Zunner. Nürnberg 1709. (Gewerbemuseum Basel.) Plates 138 and 139.

LAOPERI
NA
di Ludouico Vicentino, da
imparare di
scriue=
re
littera can=
cellares=
cha

A chiunque uole imparare scriuere lra
corsiua, o sia cancellaresca conuiene
osseruare la sottoscritta norma
&
Primieramente imparerai di fare que=
sti dui tratti, cioe - ·
dali quali se principiano tutte
le
littere cancellare=
sche,
Deli quali dui tratti l'uno é piano et
grosso,
l'altro é acuto et sotti
le
come qui tu puoi uedere notato

PLATE 1: Vicentino, Rome, 1522

LITERARUM
latinarũ, quas
Italicas, cursoriasque
vocat, scribendarũ
ratio

cuspis, qua in trãsuersum pergit
longius abeat, ac tum sursum bre
uißimè reductum circularem ar
cum in superiorem coniu=
gatam demittat talẽ,
quem mediocris ac descendentis
lineę initiũ terminet sic

Restat & cuius formatio talis
est In superiore coniugata
pingito retrogrado ordine o literæ
caput, queq; sequitur cir
cumductio nusquàm
à circulari figura recedat, Usq;
dum in tenuissimã, vel in tenui
orem ipsius v lineam de
ducta fuerit, sic

PLATE 2: Mercator, Antwerp, 1540

Alterius cōbinationis sunt ct
st ct st ſt ſp ſſp ß
& æ ae œ, quarum plures
ex literarum figuratione
facillimam compositione
habent.
In ct st ſp connectens
linea consideranda est.
Hęc ab extremo
c aut s rostro leuorsum molliter
circumlata in transuersam pro
dit lineam, eamq; rectam; quę
dextro fine vel recta vel sursū
recurua constanter in
p aut t literę prius
elemētum descēdat.
Hoc idem vinculum, si lasciuu

a b c d e c f g g g
g h i k k k l m n o
p p q r ſ s t v v v
x x x x x x x x
y y z z z & &
ſt st st st ct ct ct
ct ſſp ſp ſſ ß ſſ q
ff æ æ æ ę ę œ

PLATE 3: Mercator, Antwerp, 1540

& tirasi in giù co'l trauerso. ſ. dandoli la sua uolta ne'l fine. ſ. & la sua longhezza vuol esser doi corpi & doi terzi, e'l suo Taglio sarà sopra li doi Corpi. f. di modo che infino alla cima, auanzino li doi terzi, Secondo il parer mio. f. anchorche alcuni dicono uolere auanzare un corpo intero sopra il suo Taglio.

La. g. discende dal'. a. & vuol essere longa doi Corpi, dando maggior larghezza al secondo corpo che al primo, & non vi marauigliate se'l Corpo di sotto pare più longo che quello di sopra, per che par cosi per esser piu largo, come uedete.

& si tirano in giù co'l Trauerso. ı. lasciandoli il suo Taglietto nel fine de la lettera, Ma auuertirete che la ligatura dell'una gamba con l'altra, si deue incominciare, passata la metà del primo Trauerso, & cosi seguirete l'altre gambe, come vedete.

La lettera. o. si forma come la. c. & si serra con un tratto alquanto curuato.

La. p. si comincia co'l Taglio. /. & tirasi giù co'l Trauerso. ı. dandoli la sua uolta nel fine. ȷ. & il corpo si forma come quello de la. b. p. auuertendo che'l principio dell'hasta sia un poco più alto del Corpo. p. per che pare che

PLATE 4: Palatino, Rome, 1544

À uolere imparare regolarmente questa
Eccellente virtu de lo Scriuere,
Qual si uoglia Sorte di
lettere, è necessa-
rio
primieramente sapere tenere ben la penna
in mano,
Senza la quale auuertenza, è impossibi-
le peruenire alla uera perfettione de lo
Scriuere.
& però auuertirete che la penna si
deue tenere con le due prime
dita appoggiandole so-
pra 'l terzo,
Per che tenendola altrimenti, Il tratto no
uerria sicuro, ma
tremolante,

O ltra di questo, la penna si deue tenere
salda in mano, co'l brac-
cio posato
Sopra
la Tauola, non la
Volteggiando ne lo Scri-
uere, Tenendola al
quanto di trauerso, Onde seco-
do la uera dispositione di essa pena
tenuta in questo modo, ne na-
scono tre tratti
naturali.
Il primo Tratto appresso Mathematici,
si diria Proportione quintupla,
per che consta di cinque
parti del taglio,

PLATE 5: Palatino, Rome, 1544

Maiuscole Cancellaresche.

Iohannes Baptista Palatinus Ciuis Roma. Scribeba.

Abbreuiature.

Iohes Bapt^ta de Palatio Scribebat.

PLATE 6: Palatino, Rome, 1544

H, or quali adunq; à tanti tui meriti
Potransi lode dar pari? Qual lauro
Ò mirto circondar à tuoi
Crini sacri di corona degna?

A a b c d e f g h i k l m n o p q
r s t u x y z Z.

&

Palatinus Romæ Scribebat
Anno Domini.
MDXXXX

Enigma

Vn Giouanetto ama vna donna bella,
Ch'ogni cosa per lei mette in oblio,
Onde alfin le si scuopre, & le fauella,
& la priega, ch'adempia 'l suo disio,
Ma tosto gli rispondr la Donzella,
& dice non hauerai già l'amor mio
S'un don primieramente non mi fai,
Che non hai, non hauerai, ne hauesti mai.

Ioannes Baptista Palatinus Roman. Ciuis Scribebat.

A aa bb cc dd ee ff gg hh ij kk ll mm nn oo pp
qq rr ß ſſ s ſt v u u x x y y z z & ℈

PLATE 7: Palatino, Rome, 1544

Eglie manifesto Egregio lettore, che le lettere Can=
cellaresche sono de uarie sorti, si come poi ueder
nelle scritte tabelle, le quali io scritto con mesura
e arte, Et per satisfatione de cui apitisse una
sorte, et cui unaltra, Io io scritto questa altra
uariatione de lettere la qual uolendo imparare
osserua la regula del sottoscritto Alphabeto :

A a. b. c. d. e e. ff. g. h. i. k. l. m. n. o. p. p.
q. q. r. s. ſ. t. u. x. y. z. &.

Le lettere cancellaresche sopranominate se fanno tonde
longe large tratizzate e non tratizzate ET per che io
io scritto questa uariacione de lettera la qual im=
pareraj secundo li nostri precetti et opere

A a a b. c. d. e e. f. g. h. i. k. l. m. n. o. p. q. r. s. ſ. t. u. x. y. z. &.

Plate 8: Tagliente, Venice, 1531

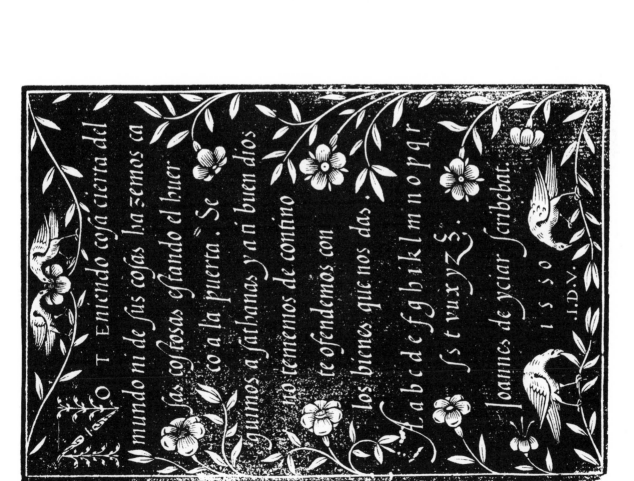

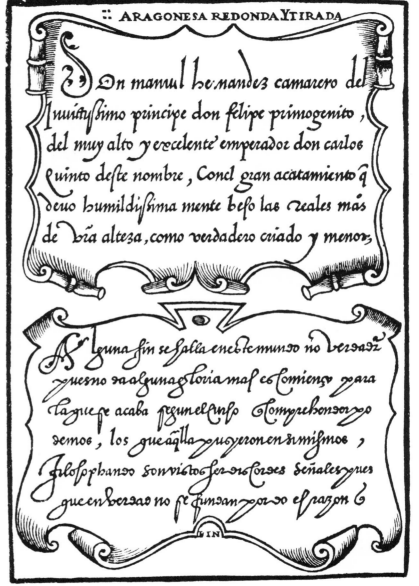

PLATE 9: Yciar, Saragossa, 1550

PLATE 10: Yciar, Saragossa, 1550

Plate ii: Yciar, Saragossa, 1550

PLATE 12: Yciar, Saragossa, 1550

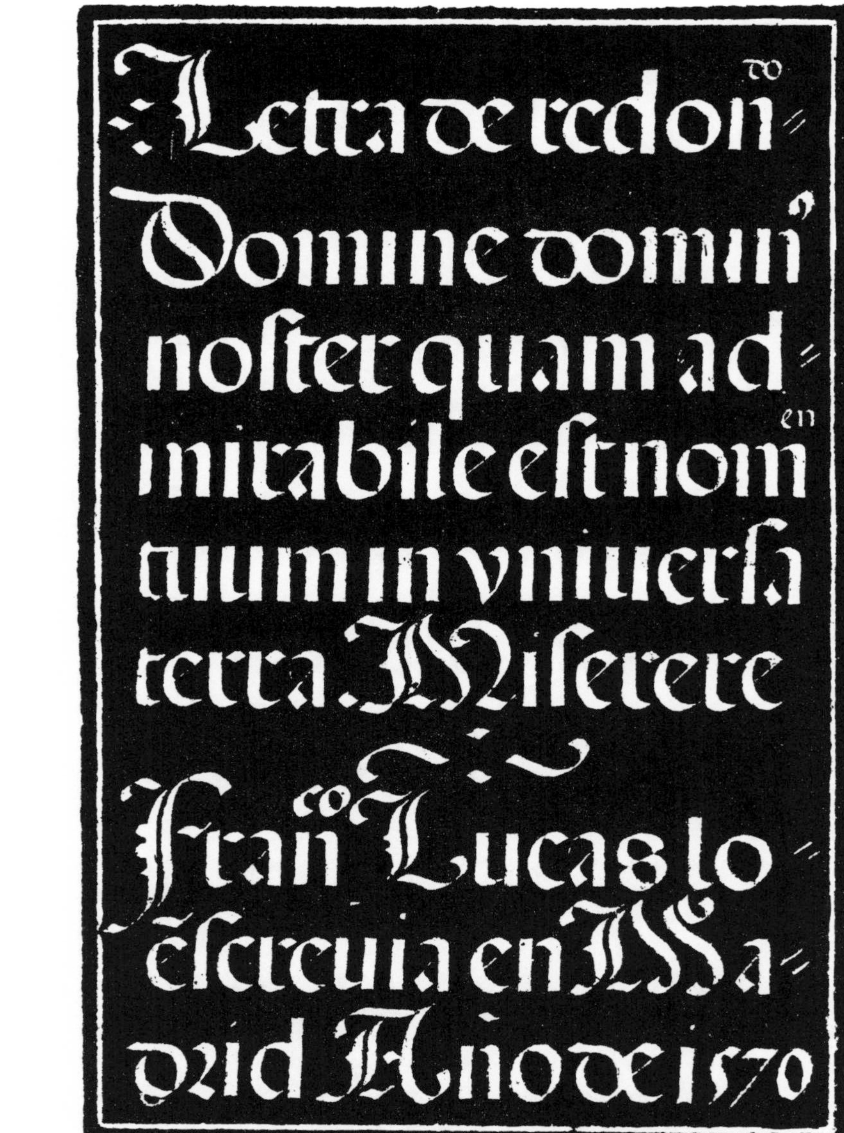

PLATE 13: Yciar, Saragossa, 1550 (*left*); Lucas, Madrid, 1580 and 1608 (*right*)

abc, con sus principi-
os

Fr.co Lucas lo escreuia
en Madrid año de 1570

Redondillo

En el campo me meti
a lidiar con mi desseo,
comigo mismo peleo
defiendame Dios de mi
Si yo mismo me doy
guerra, y

Fran. Lucas. Año 1570

PLATE 14: Lucas, Madrid, 1580 and 1608

Redondilla llana mas pequeña:

La virtud es ganancia que nunca se pierde, rio que no se passa, mar que no se nauega, fuego que nunca se apaga, tesoro que jamas fenece, exercito que nunca se vence, carga que nunca pesa, espia q̃ siempre buelue, guarda que no se engaña:

Fran. Lucas lo escreuia en Madrid Año de MDLXX:

PLATE 15: Lucas, Madrid, 1580 and 1608

LETRA AN=
~: tigua :~

Nunc dimittis ſeruum tu=
um domine ſecundum ver
bum tuum in pace. Qui avi=
derunt occuli mei ſalutare
tuum. Quod paraſti ante=
~: ſa :~

Fran^co^ Lucas lo eſcreuia en=
Madrid Año De. M. D.
~: LXX :~

LETRA DEL:~
~: griſo :~

Domine dominus noſter qua
admirabile eſt nomen tuum
in vniuerſa terra. Miſericor
dias domini in eternum can=
tabo. In generatione et gene=
~: ra :~

Fran^co^ Lucas lo eſcreuia en
Madrid Año de M. D.
~ . Lxx :~

PLATE 16: Lucas, Madrid, 1580 and 1608

:abc con sus principios

Fran.co Lucas me escreuia en madrid año 1570

:Otro abc sin principios

Fran.co Lucas lo escreuia en Madrid año de 1570

PLATE 17: Lucas, Madrid, 1580 and 1608

Bastarda grande llana

Obsecrote domina sancta
Maria mater Dei pietate
plenissima, summi regis fi-
lia, mater gloriosissima, ma
ter orphanorum, consola
tio desolatorum, via erran-
tium
Fran.co Lucas lo escreuia en
Madrid año de M D LXX

Bastarda llana Mas peque-
ña

Cantate domino canticum nouum: can
tate domino omnis terra. Cantate domi
no et benedicite nomini eius: annuntia
te de die in diem salutari eius. Annun-
tiate inter gentes gloriam eius: in omni
bus populis mirabilia eius. Quoniam
magnus dominus et laudabilis nimis:
terribilis est super omnes Deos. Quoniam omnes dij gentium dæmonia
Dominus
Fran.co Lucas Lo escreuia En
Madrid Año De M D LXX

PLATE 18: Lucas, Madrid, 1580 and 1608

BASTARDO LLANO DE CARTAS

Preguntado Apolonio: segun cuenta Filostrato: qual fuesse el mas rico hombre del mundo, respondio el mas rico es el mas sabio. Preguntado despues quien fuesse el mas pobre, respondio que el mas ignorante. Fue sentencia por cierto digna de tal persona: la verdad dela qual cada ora vemos por experiencia. Porque el hombre sabio arrodillando en muchos varios casos dela fortuna se tiene, y el hombre ignorante en qual Quiera

Fran.^co Lucas Lo escreuia en Madrid Año de M.D.

lxx

ABC Mayusculas de Bastardo

A A A A B B B B C C
D D D D E E E F F F
F F G G G G H H H I I
I I L L L M M M M M M M
N N N H H H O O P P P
P Q Q Q R R R R R S S S
T T T V V V V X X Y Y
Z Z
FRAN.^co LUCAS LO
escreuia en Madrid Año de M D lxx

PLATE 19: Lucas, Madrid, 1580 and 1608

Frate Vespasiano Amphyareo.

La grandissima beneuolenza qual porto al nostro commune amico, Giouan batt^a
Ciardi. S. Christofano amantissimo, mi ha constretto di mutar proposito; impero=
chè sendomi quasi chè deliberato di non uolere intagliare nell'opra mia altra sor=
te di lettra che quella Bastarda tanto fauorita, pure sapendo poi quanta incli=
natione egli habbi alla mia Cancellaresca della quale tanto sollecitaua gli amati
figliuolini, in sua gratificatione le presenti pollice sono date in luce, ne altro occorr.
se non che a V. R. et alla humanissima cortesia sua infinitamente mi raccom.

Al suo Giouan Battista ciardi.

PLATE 20: Vespasiano, Venice, 1564

A A B C D E F G J K L M N O P Q R S T V.

Se dal mondo sempre non fussero state in somma ueneratione le sacrosante lettre humanissimo lettore non haurebbono gli antichi cosi longamente conteso à cui douesse donar la palma della inuentione di esse Imperoche alcuni attribuiuano q̄a gloria al Magnanimo Hercule, alt.i a Nicostrata od'à Carmenta, altri a Palamede nella guerra Troiana, molti a Numa Pompilio à cui erano diuine cose reuelate dalla Nimph. Egeria, & pure erano quelle dal suo principio roze, et mal formate, Pensa tu adunque di che laude siano degni q̄lli che ornate et Terse anoi le dimostrano &

A a a b b c d d e f ff g Giouan Batt. Car.mo b i j k l m n o p q r

PLATE 21: Vespasiano, Venice, 1564

A a b l b c d d e e f f g g h h k l M m n o p q r

Facilmente si comprendeno gli intimi precordij delli huomini confabulando seco, dalli cottidiani ragionamenti, dalli loro mouimenti & da altre mille sopraueni enti occa= sioni. Onde gli sapientissimi, & esperimentatissimi Philosophi insegnorono alla posteritade questi documenti, per ilche obligatissimi sempre dobbiamo essere alle memorie loro Imitando con ogni nostro studio et diligentia vigilantissimamente, quanto quelli s'affaticorono scriuere, à nostro beneficio, ornamento & spetial vti= litade, Et cosi fuggiremo ogni nota de ingratitudine qle si attribuisse alli obliuio.

& S s s st t u u v v x x y z z del frate

PLATE 22: Vespasiano, Venice, 1564

Caiissime pr, post beatissimorum pedum oscula La Santita vra sera ragguagliata
qualmente à giorni quattordeci Decembre gli R uerendissimi Et Illustrissimi Car.li
Grimano et Sadoletto noncij di uostra Santita, et di qlla beatissima Sede, nelli rg.i
di Franza et Scocia Insieme con il Clarissimo ambasciatore dello Inuittissimo et
potentissimo Senato Veneto furono á strettissimi ragionamenti con la Maestà
Christianiss, In materia delle quattro decime nouamete imposte p il sacrosanto
Concistorio in tutto il Christianesmo sopra le rendite de beneficij ecclesiastici

PLATE 23: Vespasiano, Venice, 1564

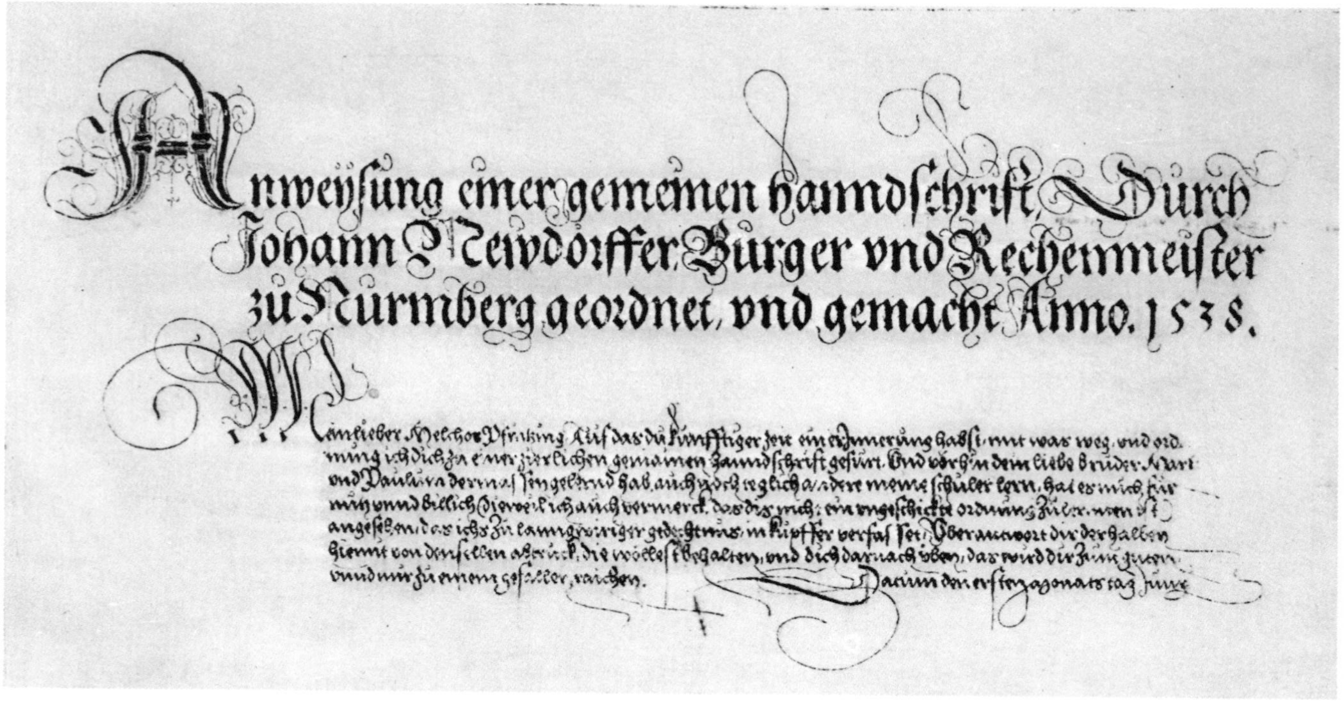

Anweysung einer gemeinen handschrift, Durch Johann Neudorffer Burger vnd Rechenmeister zu Nurmberg geordnet, vnd gemacht Anno. 1538.

PLATE 24: Neudörffer, Nuremberg, 1538

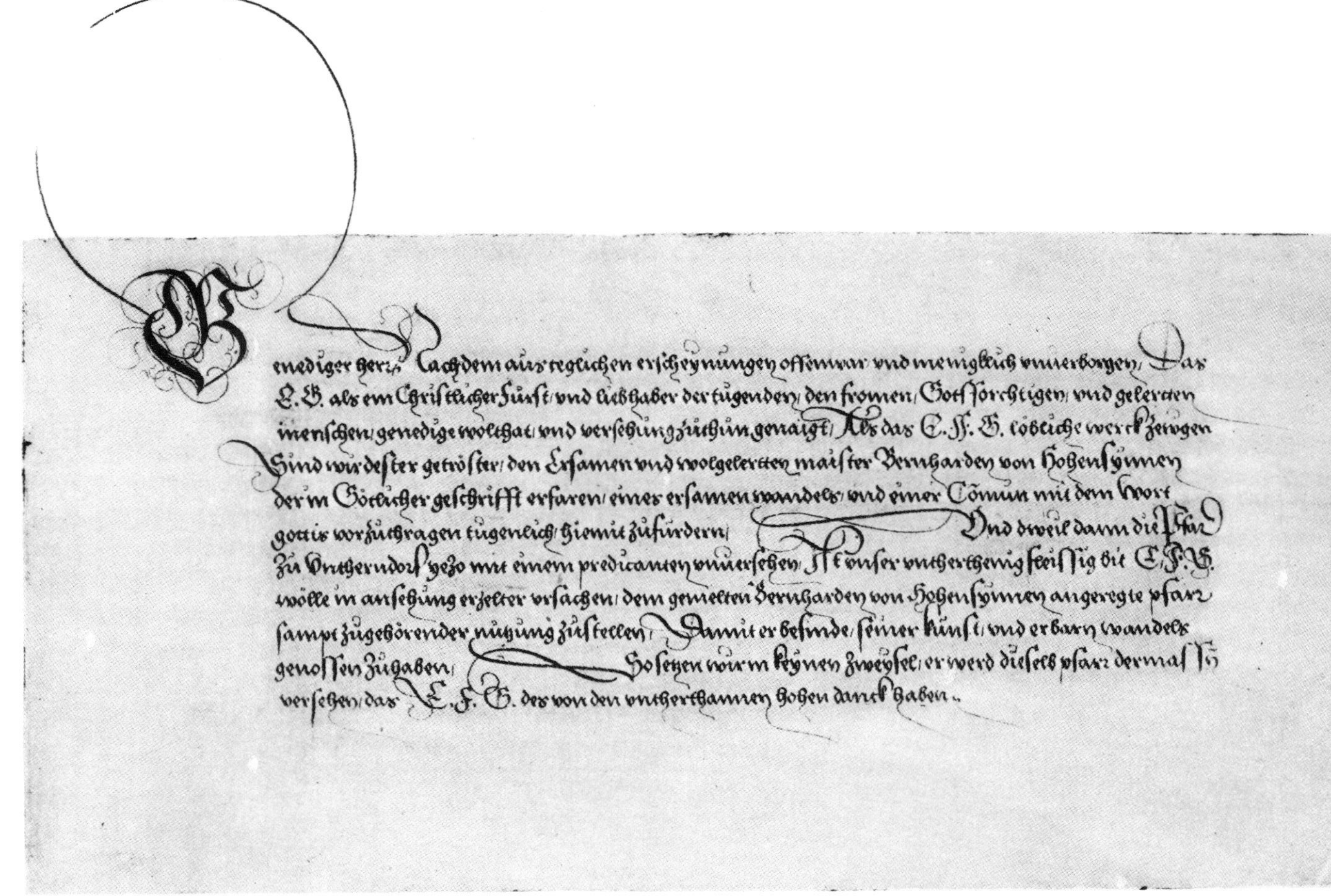
Genediger herr, Nachdem aus teglichen erscheynungen offenbar und menigklich unverborgen, Das
E.G. als ein Christlicher Fürst und liebhaber der tugenden, den fromen, Gotsförchtigen, und gelerten
menschen genedige wolthat und versehung zuthun genaigt, Als das E.F.G. löbliche werck zeugen
Sind wir dester getröster, den Ersamen und wolgelerten maister Bernharden von Hohensymen
der in Göttlicher geschrifft erfaren, einer ersamen wandels, und einer Comun mit dem wort
gottis vorzutragen tugenlich, hiemit zufürdern, Und dweil dann die pfarr
zu Untherndorf yezo mit einem predicanten unversehen, Ist unser untherthenig fleissig bit E.F.G.
wölle in ansehung erzelter ursachen, dem gemelten Bernharden von Hohensymen angeregte pfarr
sampt zugehörender nutzung zustellen, Damit er befinde seiner kunst, und erbarn wandels
genossen zuhaben, So setzen wir in keynen zweyfel, er werd dieselb pfarr dermas zu
versehen, das E.F.G. des von den untherthanen hohen danck haben.

PLATE 25: Neudörffer, Nuremberg, 1538

Damit du aber aigentlich sehen, vnnd lernen mogst. wie sich yetzuerzaichende figuren sich mit allen iren linien beschliessen, vnnd mit den zweyen ecken. oder spitzen sampt der schneiden zusammengefugt werden. Wil ich dir dieselben mit einer federn, die nit mer dann zwen punct spitzen hat, vnnd das feld mit dinten nicht ausfult fur machen. Mit diser ausgeschwaiften federn werden im zierlichen schreiben schöne ding gemacht vnnd erfunden. Es werden auch, die grossen alten Lateinischen buchstaben (deren auslegung ich auch in einem sondern buchlein mit fleis gesucht vnnd gemacht hab) von etlichen den pesten schreibern in welschland mit diser federn gezogen. Vnnd darnach erst mit dinten, farben, oder goldgrunnd ausgefult Vnnd sind dis die holen superfities oder fertzug.

14. 15. 16. 17. 18. 19. 20. 21. 22. 23. 24.

25. 26. 27. 28. 29. 30. 31. 32. 33.

Mit gespaltner federn.
sunst gabelfeder genand

PLATE 26: Neudörffer, Nuremberg, 1538

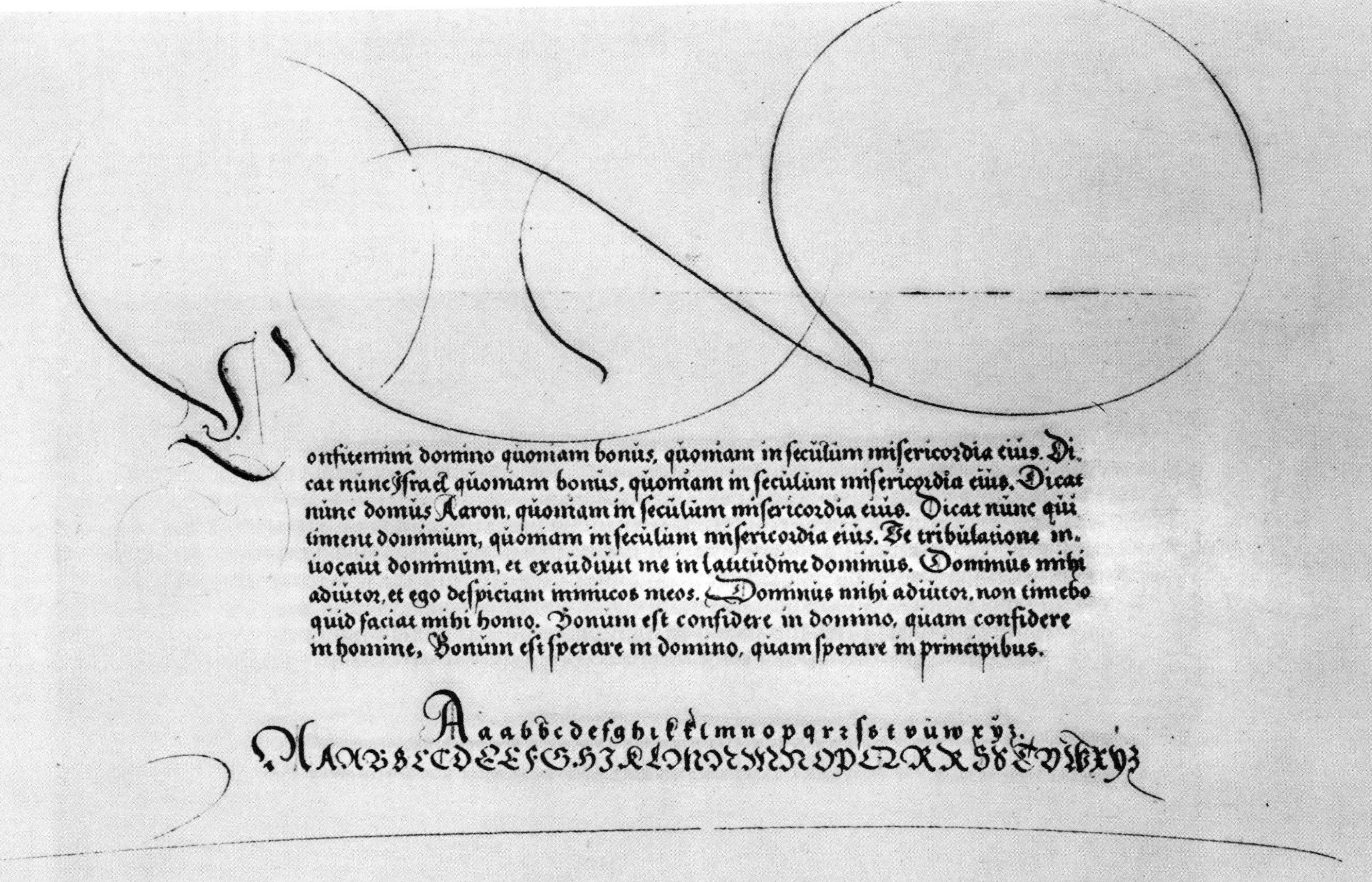

PLATE 27: Neudörffer, Nuremberg, 1538

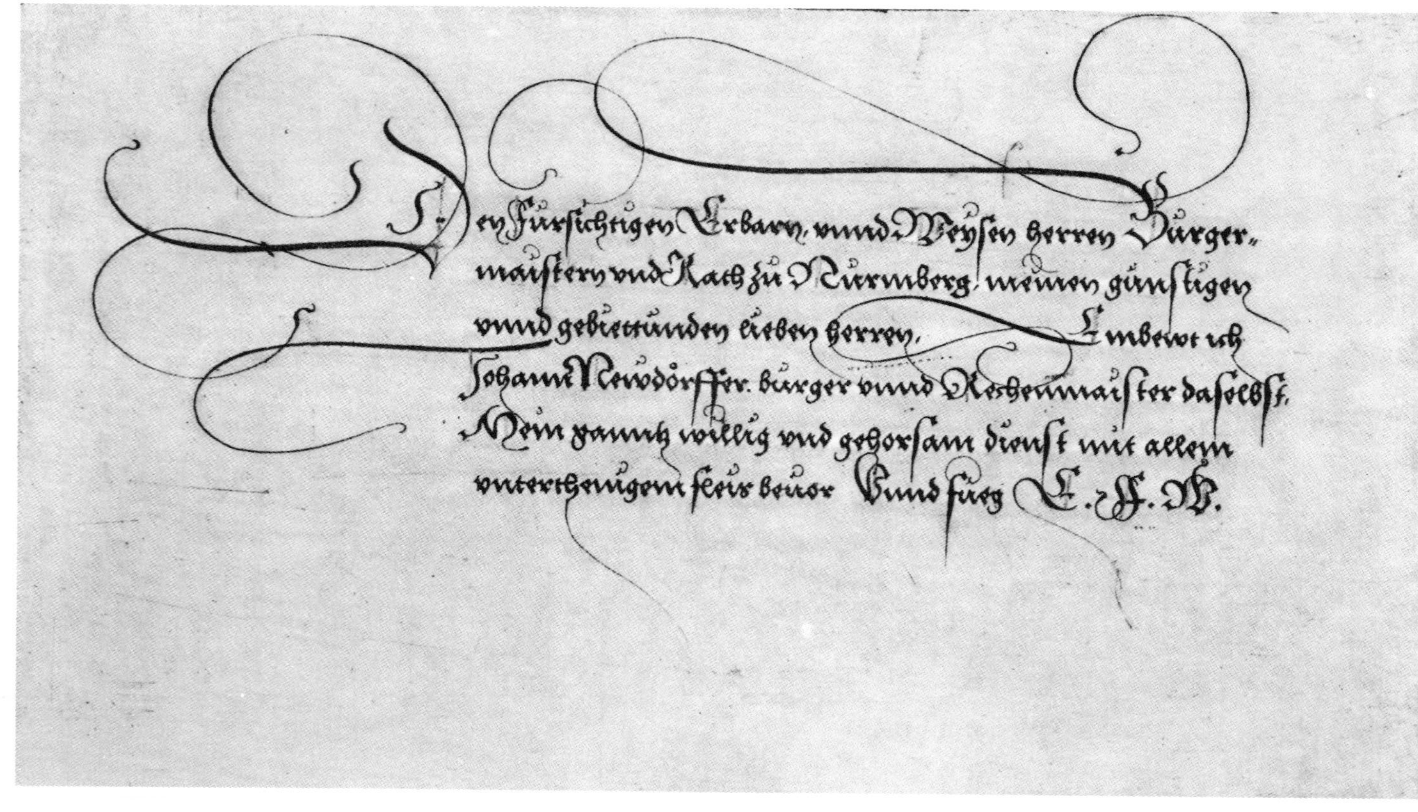

Den Fürsichtigen Erbarn vnnd Weysen herren Burger-
maistern vnd Rath zu Nürmberg meinen günstigen
vnnd gebiettunden lieben herren. Embeut ich
Johann Neudörffer burger vnnd Rechenmaister daselbst.
Mein gantz willig vnd gehorsam dienst mit allem
vnterthenigem fleis beuor Vnnd fueg E. F. W.

PLATE 28: Neudörffer, Nuremberg, 1538

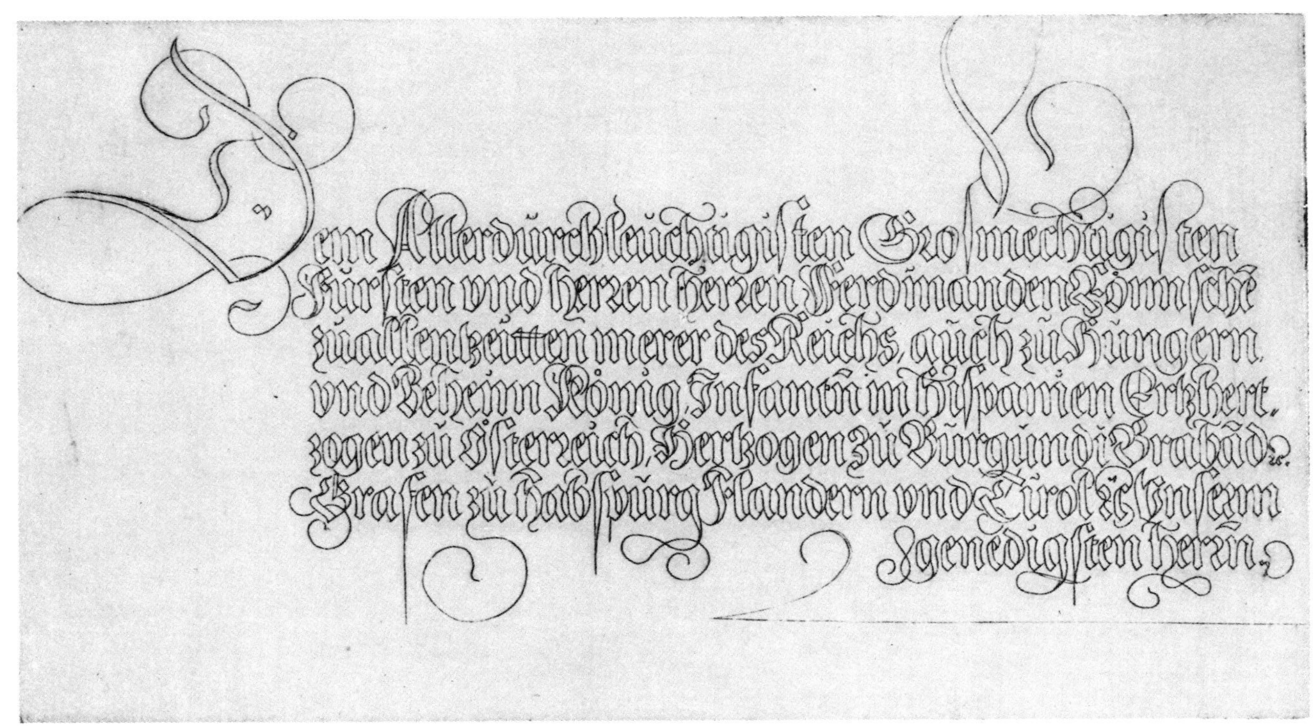

Dem Allerdürchleüchtigisten Grosmechtigisten
Fürsten vnd herren herren Ferdinanden Römischẽ
zu allen zeitten merer des Reichs, auch zu Hungern
vnd Behemn König Infantẽ in Hispanien Ertzhert-
zogen zu Österreich, Herzogen zu Bürgundi Brabãd ꝛc.
Grafen zu Habspürg Flandern vnd Tirol ꝛc. Unserm
genedigisten herren.

PLATE 29: Neudörffer, Nuremberg, 1538

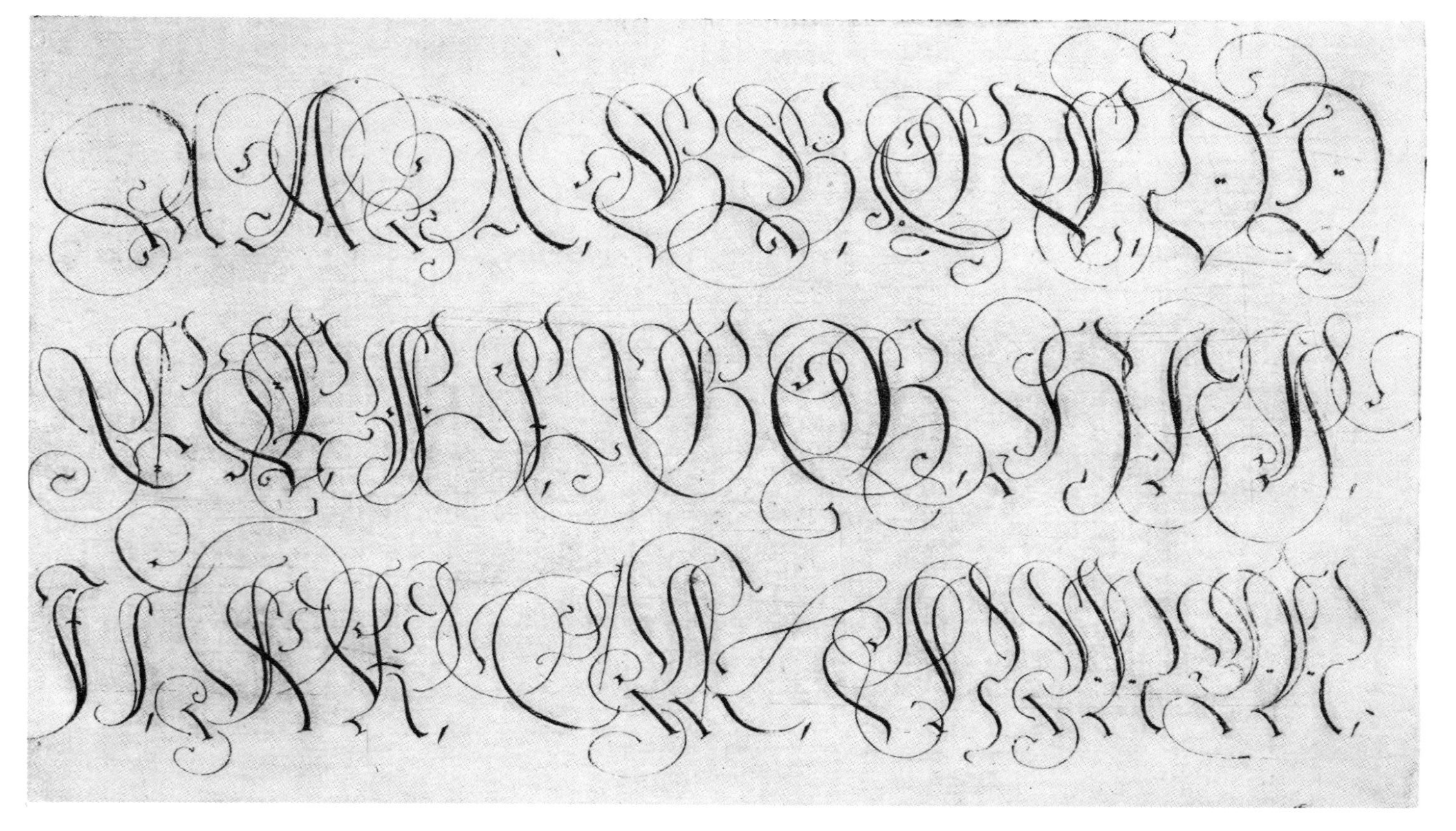

PLATE 30: Neudörffer. Nuremberg, 1538

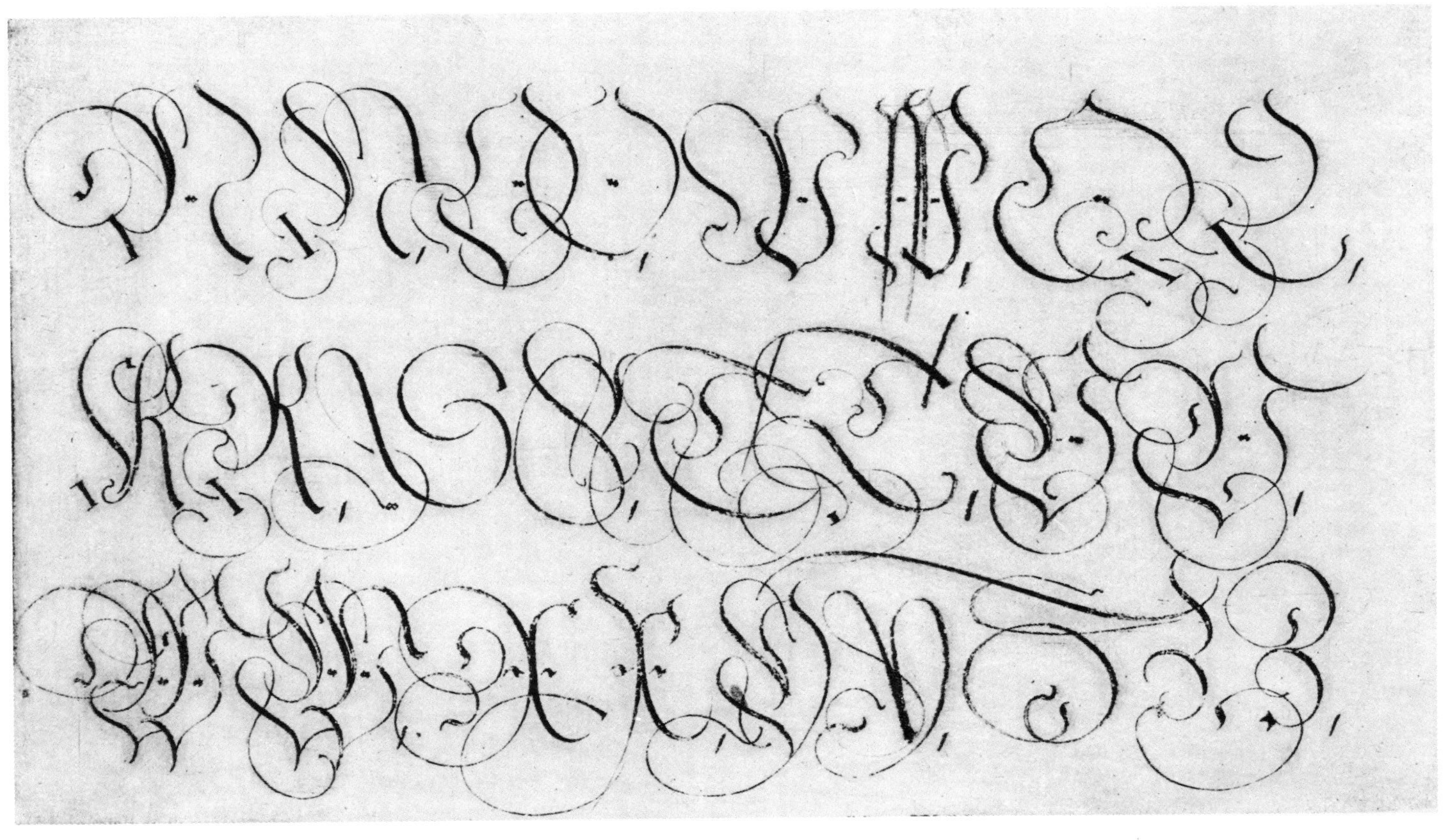

Plate 31: Neudörffer, Nuremberg, 1538

Plate 32: Neudörffer, Nuremberg, 1538

FVGITE FORNICATIONEM, OMNE ENIM PEC-
CATVM QVODCVNQ FECERIT HOMO, EXTRA
CORPVS EST; QVI AVTEM FORNICATVR, IN
CORPVS SVVM PECCAT, AN NESCITIS, QVO-
NIAM MEMBRA VESTRA TEMPLVM SVNT SPI-
RITVS SANCTI, QVI IN VOBIS EST, QVEM HA-
BETIS À DEO? ET NON ESTIS VESTRI, EMPTI
ENIM ESTIS PRECIO, GLORIFICATE ET POR-
TATE DEVM IN CORPORE VESTRO ET IN SPI-
RITV VESTRO, QVÆ SVNT DEI, I. CORIN: VI.
NOLITE ERRARE, NEQ FORNICARII, NEQVE
IDOLIS SERVIENTES, NEQ ADVLTERI, NEQ
MASCVLORVM CONCVBITORES, NEQ FVRES,
NEQ AVARI, ETC, POSSIDEBVNT REGNVM DEI, &c.

PLATE 33: Neudörffer, Nuremberg, 1538

Item breuis & dilucida institutio, qua pueri ad ueram & orthographica
Latinæ linguæ lectione facile pducunt. Sententiæ insignes & illustres
ex Cicerone desumptæ, ex quibus non tam bene dicendi, quàm bene uiuendi ratio petitur. Singulis autem sententijs singula subijciuntur Alphabeta, quæ
multifarium pueris scribendi, tum Latinè tum Germanicè modū proponunt.
Omnia hæc in gratiam & utilitatem studiosæ iuuentutis conscripta, insculp-
pta, & impressa per Vrbanum Wyss Tigurinum. Anno Domini. 1549.

PLATE 34: Wyss, Zurich, 1549

Nihil est tam aptūm ad iūs, conditionē-
uē naturæ, quàm lex, sine qua nec domūs
ūlla, nec ciuitas, nec gens, nec hominum
ūllū gen, stare, nec rex natūra omnīs, nec
etiam ipse mūndūs stare potūerit. etc.

A B C D E F G H I K L M N
O P Q R S T U W X Y Z

PLATE 35: Wyss, Zurich, 1549

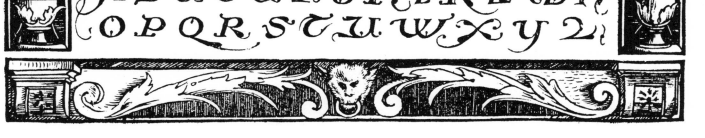

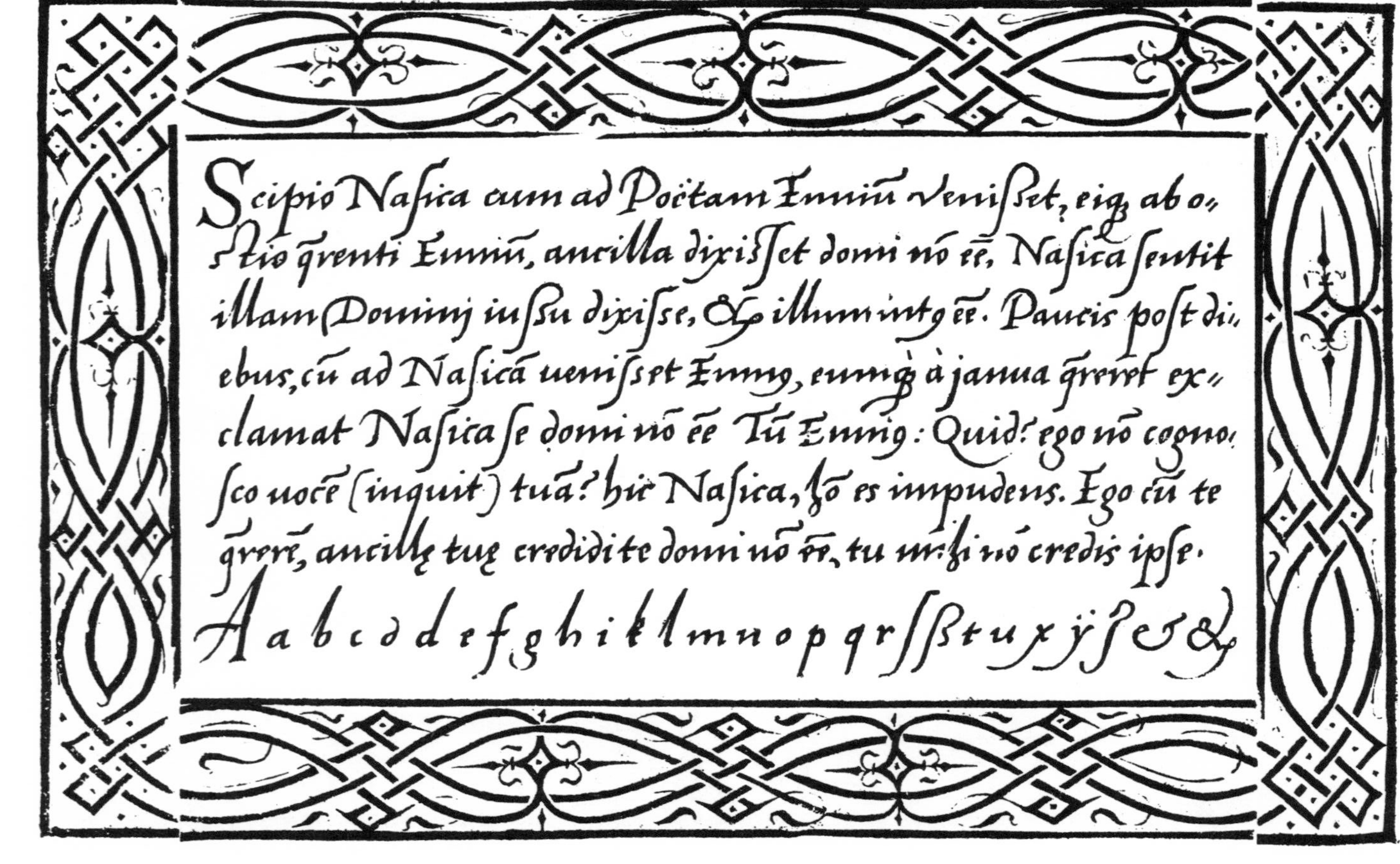

PLATE 36: Wyss, Zurich, 1549

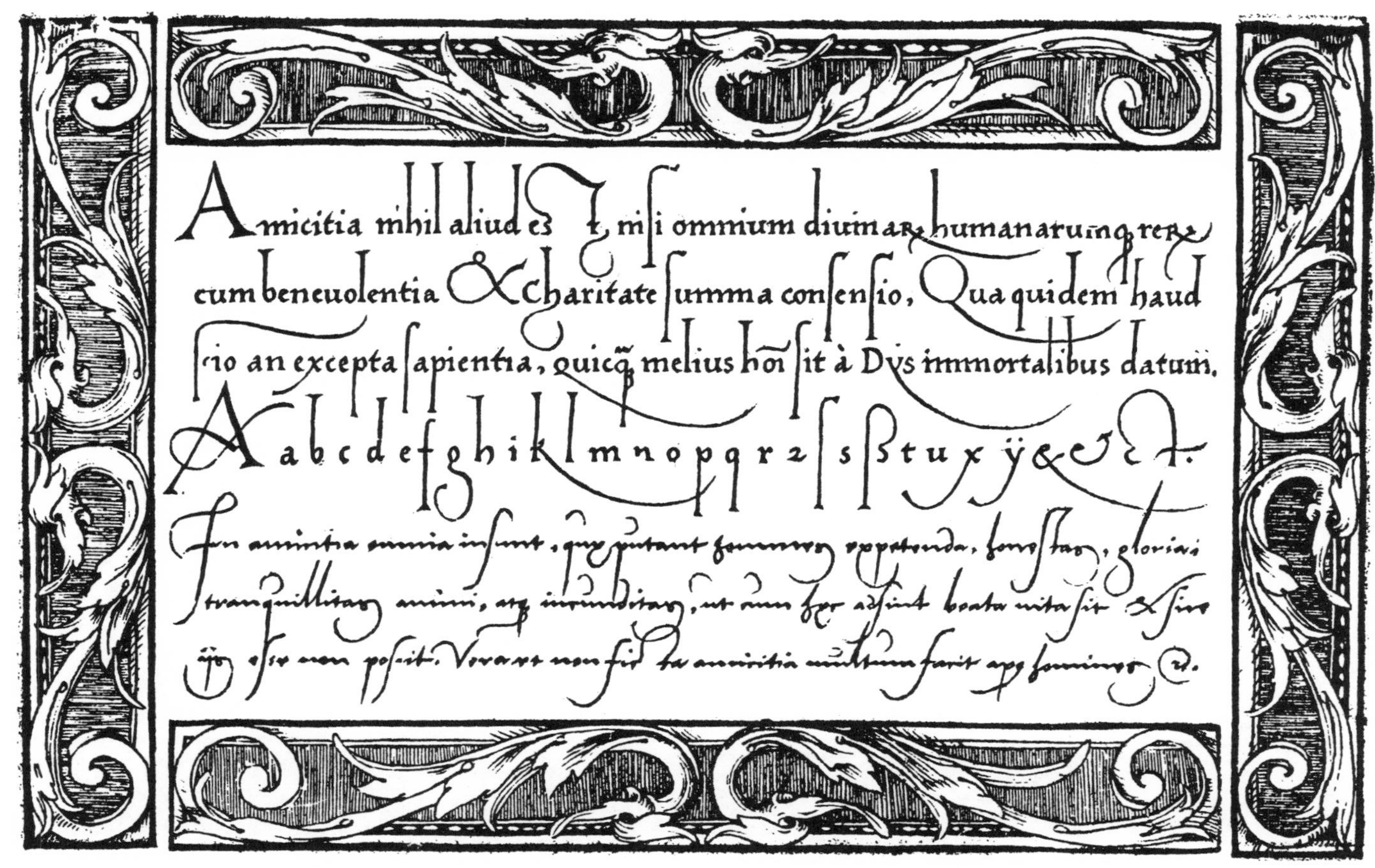

PLATE 37: Wyss, Zurich, 1549

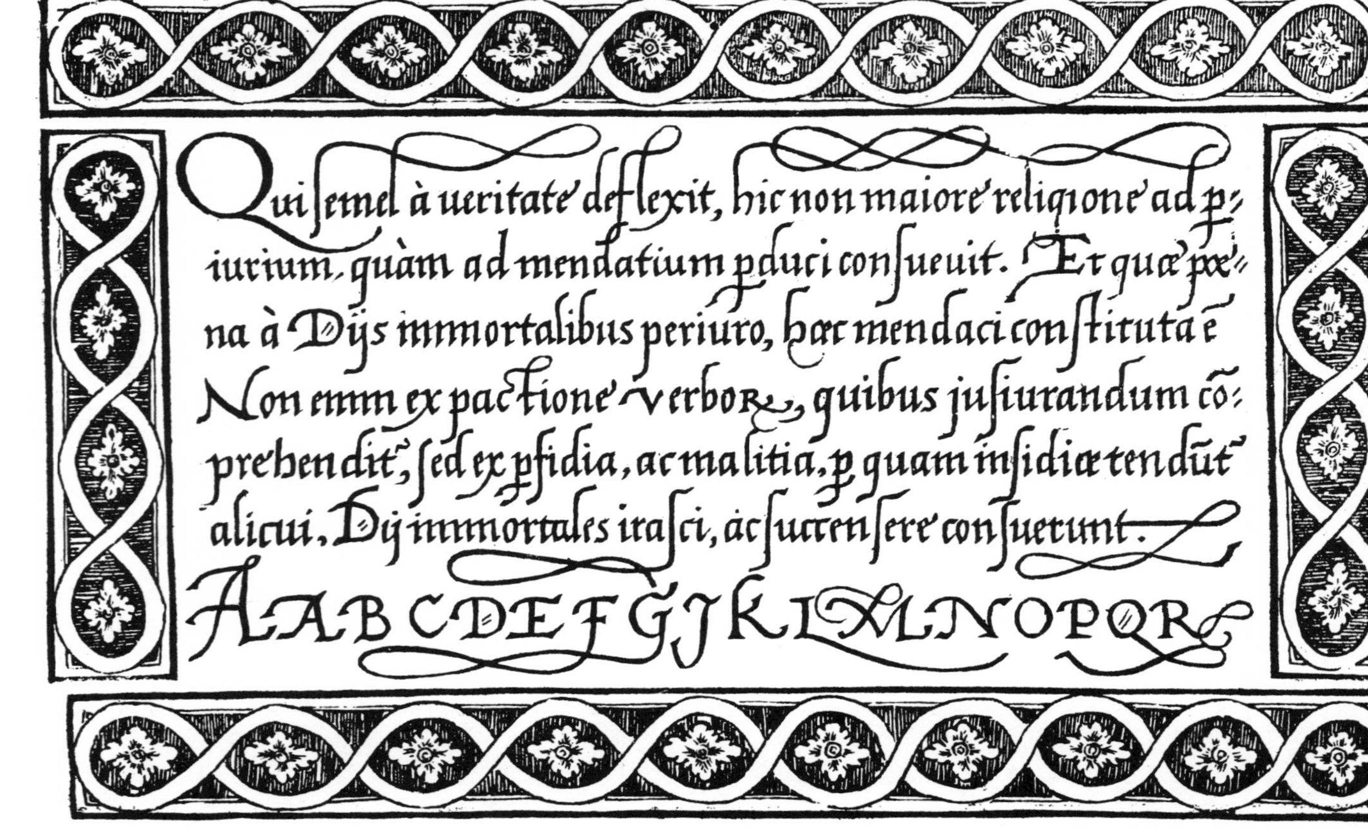

PLATE 28: Wyss, Zurich, 1549

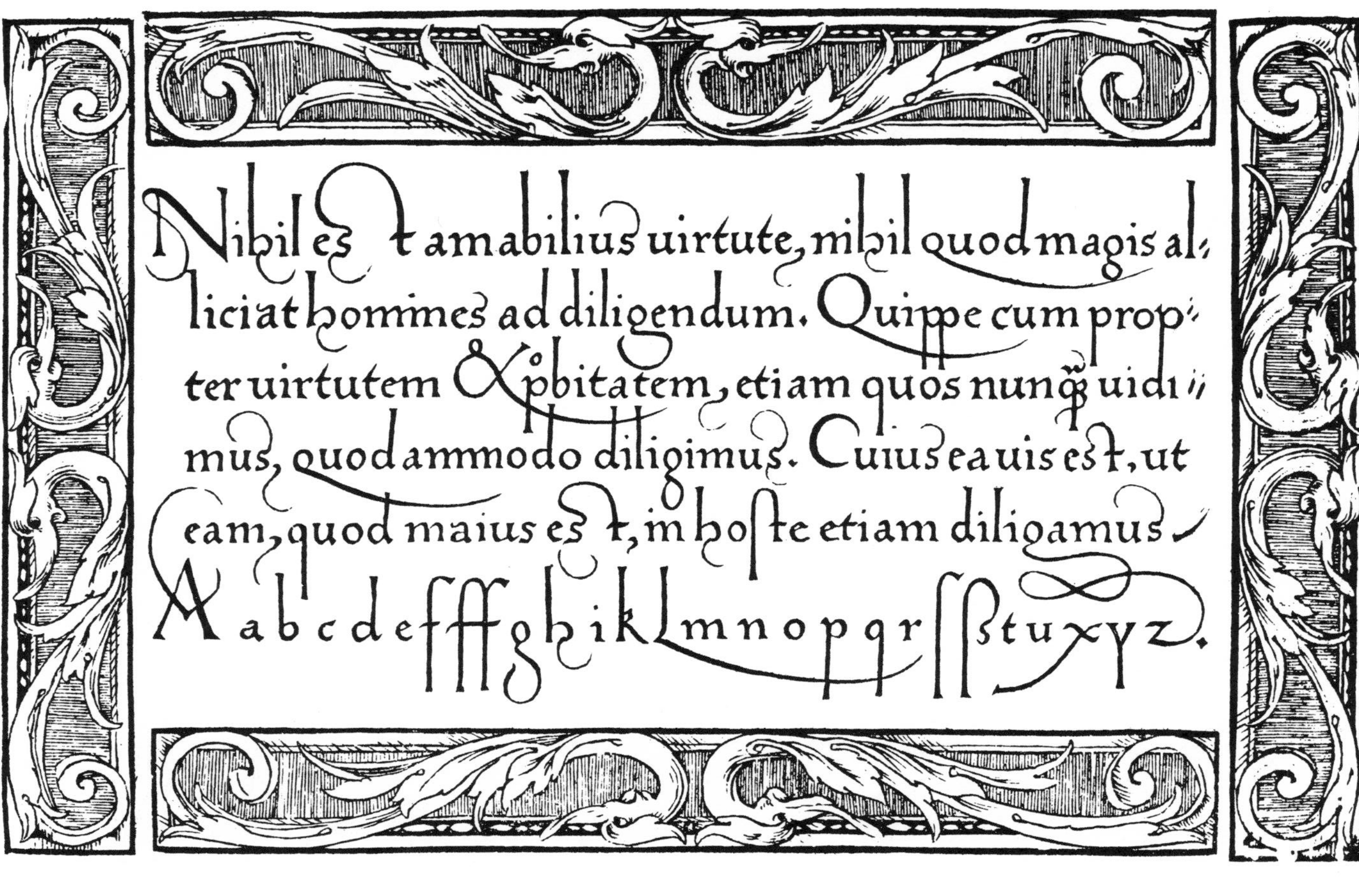

Nihil est amabilius uirtute, nihil quod magis al-
liciat homines ad diligendum. Quippe cum prop-
ter uirtutem & probitatem, etiam quos nunquam uidi-
mus, quodammodo diligimus. Cuius ea uis est, ut
eam, quod maius est, in hoste etiam diligamus.
A a b c d e f ff ff g h i k l m n o p q r ſ ſſ t u x y z.

PLATE 39: Wyss, Zurich, 1549

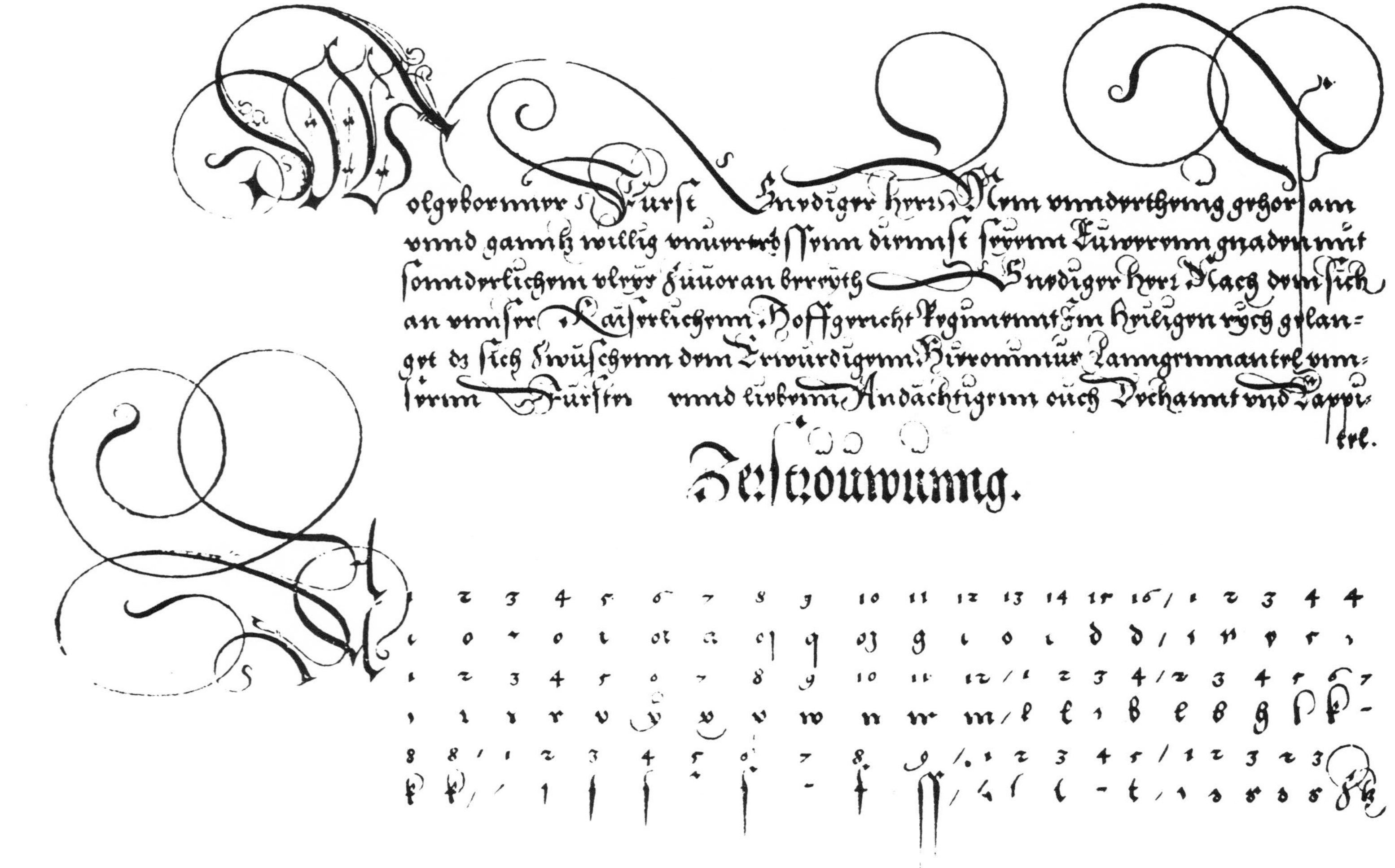

PLATE 40: Stymmer, Zurich, 1549

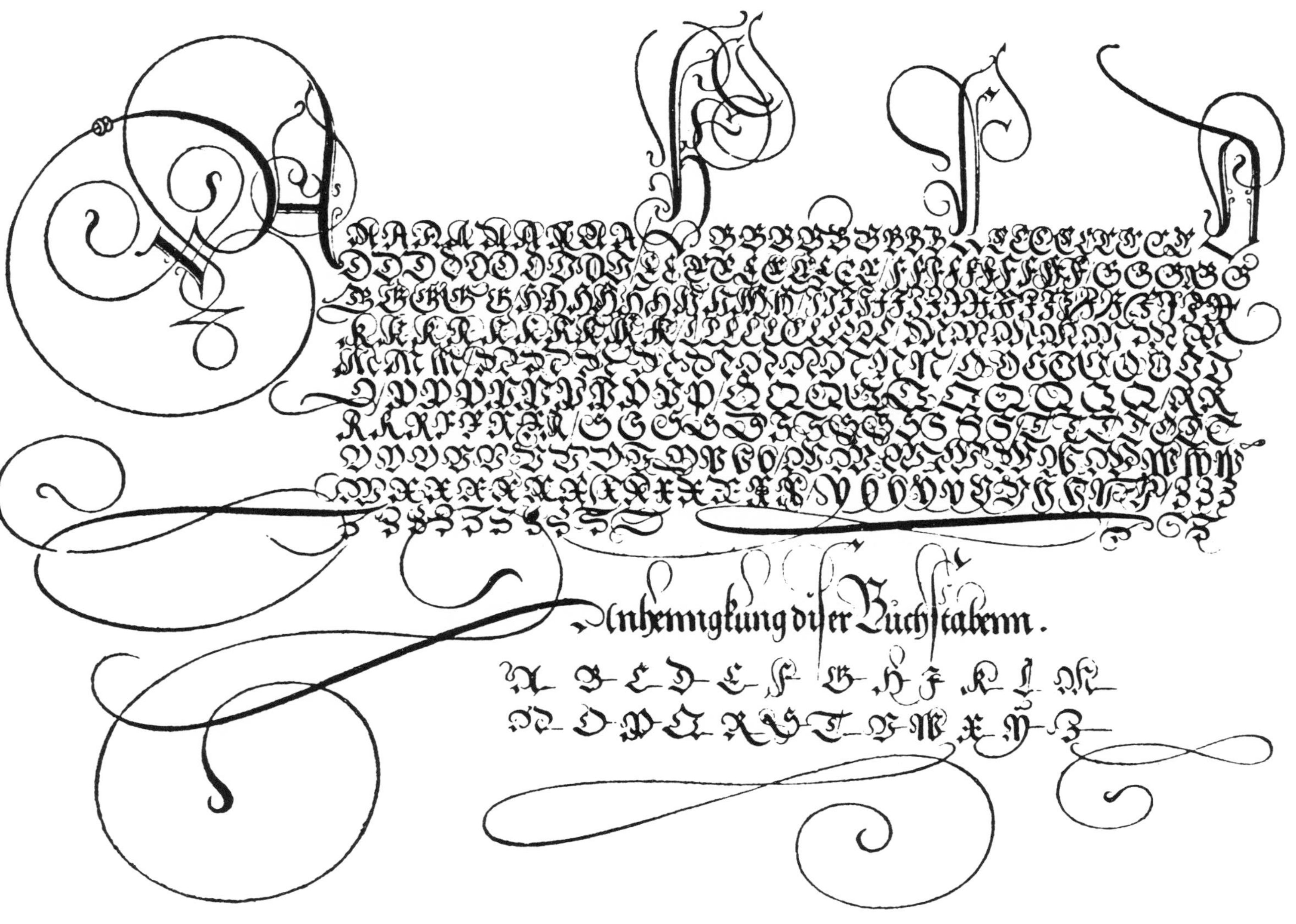

PLATE 41: Stymmer, Zurich, 1549

PLATE 42: Neff, Cologne, 1549

PLATE 43: Neff, Cologne, 1549

PLATE 44: Neff, Cologne, 1549

PLATE 45: Neff, Cologne, 1549

THESAVRARIVM
ARTIS SCRIPTORIAE ET
Cancellariæ Scribarumqꝫ Clenodium pretiosum Libellus plane aureus varia ex vero deprompta fūdamento scripta continens
antea non visa
nunc primum in lucem ædita
CASPARE NEVIO COLONIÆ AGRIPPINÆ Scriba & Arithmetico authore Anno redeptoris nostri
1549.

PLATE 46: Neff, Cologne, 1549

Scripta hoc in Thesaurario contenta sunt Latina Italica
Gallica Germanica Brabatica & Anglica

Vbiorum Coloniæ Agrippinæ cælatum & impressum Impensis
Casparis Vopelij Medeb. Mathematum professoris
Cum Gratia & priuilegio Cæsariæ Maiestatis ad decennium

PLATE 47: Neff, Cologne, 1549

CHARACTERES

quos vulgo antiquos. Romanos appellant.

Quæstus est magnus pietas cum animo sua sorte contento. Nihil enim intulim⁹ in hunc mundum, videlicet nec efferre quicquam possumus, sed habentes alimēta & quibus tegamur, his contenti erimus. Cæterum, qui volunt ditescere, incidūt in tentationem & laqueum & cupiditates multas, stultas ac noxias, quæ demergunt homines in exitium & interitum. Siquidem radix omnium malorum est studium pecuniæ, quam quidam, dum appetunt, aberrauerunt à fide & seipsos implicuerunt doloribus multis. Tu vero homo Dei ista fuge, sectare &c.

A a b c d e f g h i k l m n o p q r ſ s ſſ t u v x y z. &

A ABCDEFGHIKLMNOPQRSTVXYZZ.

PLATE 48: Neff, Cologne, 1549

ANTIQVI ROMANI, IACENTI MODO.

Induite, tanquam electi Dei sancti ac dilecti, viscera miserationum, benignitatē modestiam, mansuetudinem, lenitatem sufferentes vos inuicem & condonantes vobis, mutuo, si quis aduersus aliquem habuerit querelam, quemadmodum & Christus condonauit vobis, ita & vos. Super omnia autem hæc charitatem, quæ est vinculum perfectionis. Et pax Dei palmā ferat in cordibus vestris, in quam

PENDENTI FORMA.

Sermo Christi inhabitet in vobis opulenter cum omni sapientia. Doceteq; et cō monete vos inuicem cantionibus et laudibus & cantilenis spiritualibus, cum gratia canentes in corde vestro Domino. Et quicquid egeritis sermone aut facto omnia in nomine Domini Iesu facite, gratias agentes Deo & Patri p illum. Vxores subditę estote proprijs viris, sicuti conuenit in Domino. &c.

PLATE 49: Neff, Cologne, 1549

HI CHARACTERES IN ROMA-
na Cancellaria usurpantur

Reginam illam procacium uitiorum Auaritia fuge, cui cuncta crimina detestabili deuotione famulantur, Quę quidem Auaritia studium pecunię habet, quam nemo sapiens concupiuit: Ea quasi malis venenis imbuta, corpus animumque virilem effeminat & neque copia neque inopia minuitur. Hoc Excellentis est sapientię hominem sui ipsius habere notitiam. Nec ex dilectione quam habet in seipso fallatur & bonum se repute, cum non sit. Potens quippe est homo suos quosque actus dirigere seipsum si agnouerit.

A a B b c C D d e E F f G g b H i J k K l L M m N n o P

p Q q r R s ſ S t T u v V x X y Z z & R. r

A A B C D E F G H I K L M N O P Q R S T V X Y Z.

LATINI CHARACTERES, QVOS VVLGO SCRIPTVRAM CVRSORIAM APPELLANT.

1. Thessa. 5.

Omnes vos filij lucis estis, ac filij Diej: non sumus noctis, neq; tenebrarum. Proinde ne dormiamus, sicutj & caeterj, sed vigilemus & sobrij simus. Nam quj dormiunt nocte dormiunt, & quj inebriantur, noctu sunt ebrij. At nos quj sumus diej, sobrij simus, indutj thoracem fidej & charitatis, & pro galea spem salutis. Quoniam non constituit nos Deus, vt iram nobis concitemus, sed vt salutem consequamur per dominum nostrum Jesum Christum, quj mortuus est pro nobis, vt siue vigilemus, siue dormiamus, simul cum illo viuamus. Quapropter adhortaminj mutuo

A a b c d d e f ff g b i k l L m n o p q q r s s t v x y Z

A B C D E F G H J K L M N O P Q R S T

V X Y Z o aceddogg. l bbk. s fffss i nmiutp vxyz. st.

PLATE 51: Neff, Cologne, 1549

VNE ESCRIPTVRE FRÃ-

coyse, laquelle on vse en la Chancellerie.

Aduisez que nul ne vous surpreune par Philosophie & uaine deception, selon la traditi-
on des hommes, selon les institutions du monde, & non point selon Christ. Car en luy
toute plenté de diuinité gist corporellement: & testes complects en luy, qui est le
chef de toute Principaute & Puissance. Par lequel aussi estes circoncis de Circoncision faicte sans main, par le despouillement du corps des pechez, qui sont de la
chair, asçauoir par la Circoncision de Christ, estans en seuelis auec luy par le

A a b c d e f g h i k l m n o p q r ſ ſ s t u v x y z &.

A c acdegg l blkb. ſ ſſſſſſſ ſt ſs. ı ımntru ∨ xyz. s ſp ſſp st.

L'ESCRIPTVRE FRAN

coyse faite selon le mode pendãte, laquille on appelle Vienlle Romanie

Bienheureux sont les poures d'esprit royame des cieux est à eux Bienheureux sont ceux, qui plorent, car ils serunt consolez. Bienheureux
sont les de bonnaires, car ils possederunt la terre. Bienheureux sont-
les ceux, qui ont faim & soiff de iustice, car ils serunt saoulez. Bienheureux sont les misericordieux, car ils obtiendrunt misericorde. Bienheureux sont ceux qui sont nets de cœur, car ils verront Dieu. &c.

A a b c d e f ff g h i k l l m n o p q r s s t.
st u x y y z z st st & ct.

Ambmcmdmemfmgmhmlmkmlmnompmqmrmsmtmvmxmymzm &c.

PLATE 53: Neff, Cologne, 1549

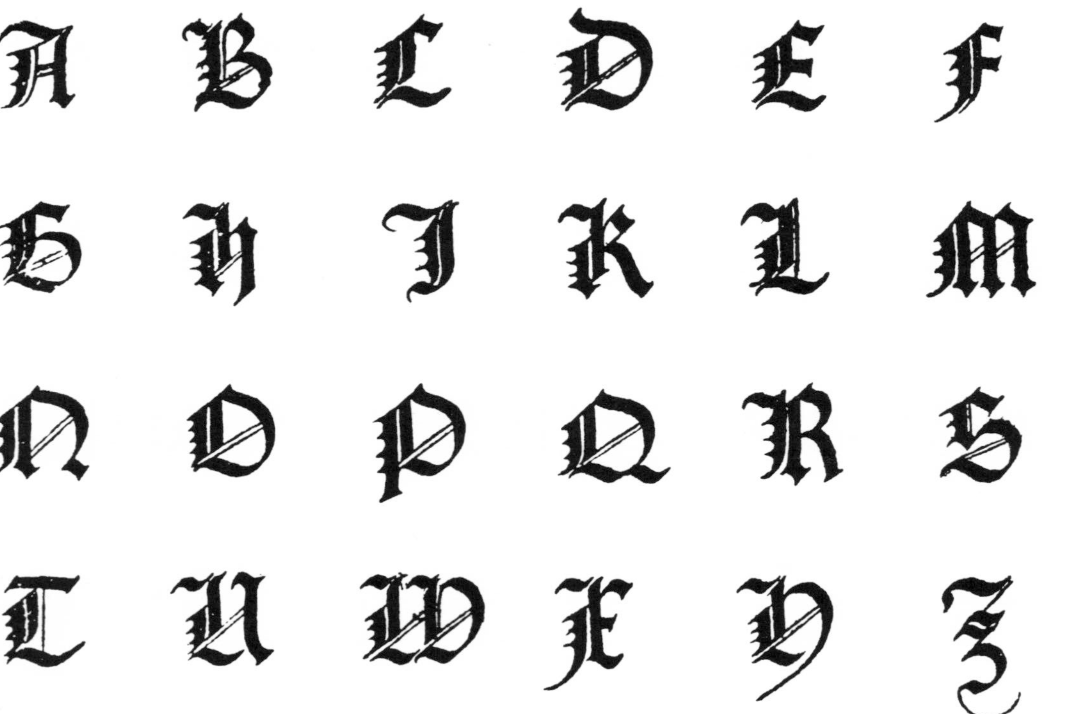

PLATE 54: Fugger, Nuremberg, 1553

Beati quorum remissæ sunt ini-
quitates, et quorum tecta sunt
peccata. Beatus vir cui non
imputavit Dominus peccatū,
nec est in spiritu eius dolus. ℞
Psalmus, xxxi.

PLATE 55: Fugger, Nuremberg, 1553

PLATE 56: Wyss, Zurich, 1562

PLATE 57: Wyss, Zurich, 1562

ABCDE
FGHIK

PLATE 58: Cresci, Venice, 1569

PLATE 59: Cresci, Venice, 1569

PLATE 60: Cresci, Venice, 1569

TVrbabunt gen-
tes et timebut
qui habitant termi-
nos à ſignis tuis: exi-
tus Io: Franc. Creſ:

PLATE 61: Cresci, Venice, 1569

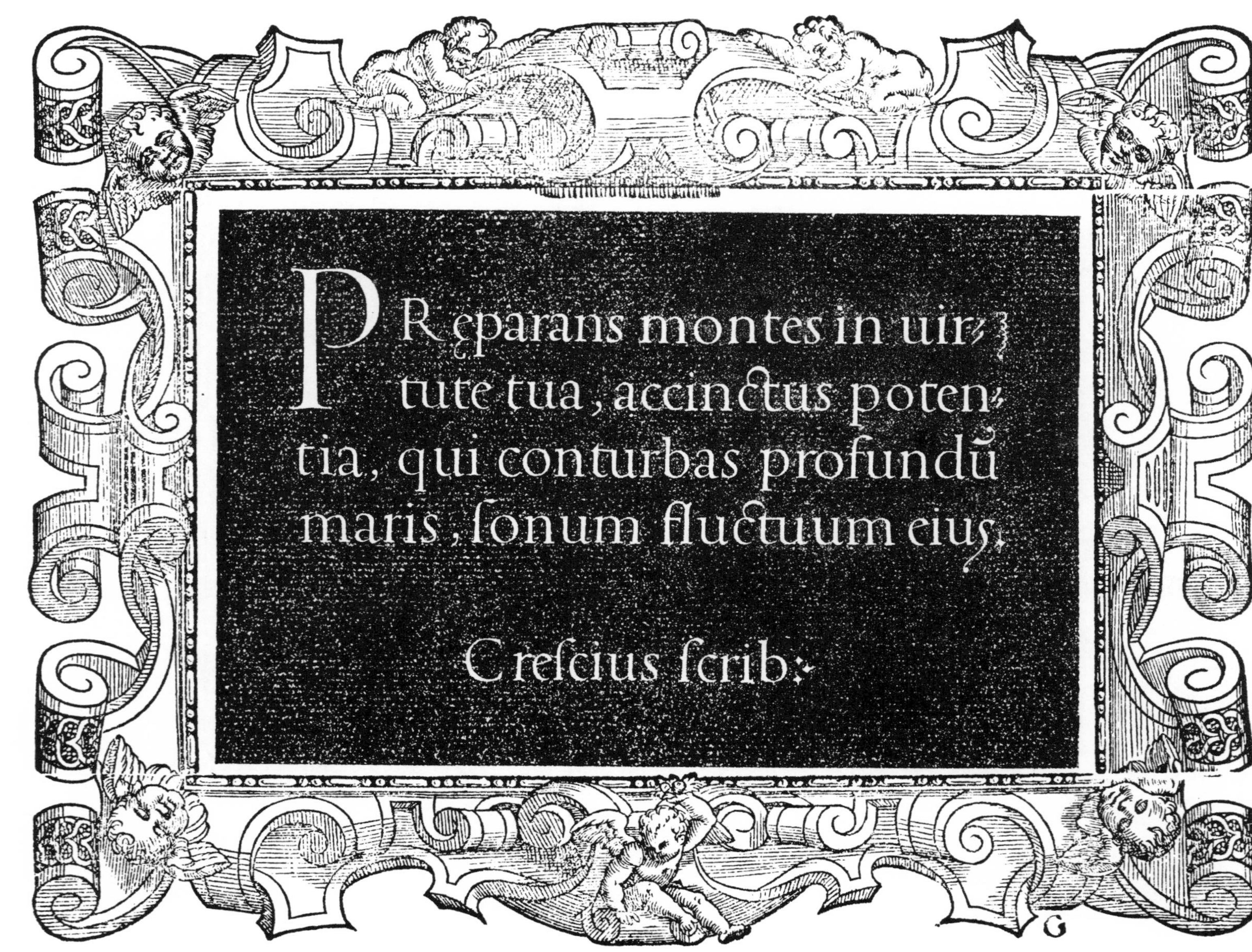
PReparans montes in uir-
tute tua, accinctus poten-
tia, qui conturbas profundũ
maris, ſonum fluctuum eius.
Creſcius ſcrib:
G

PLATE 63: Cresci, Venice, 1569

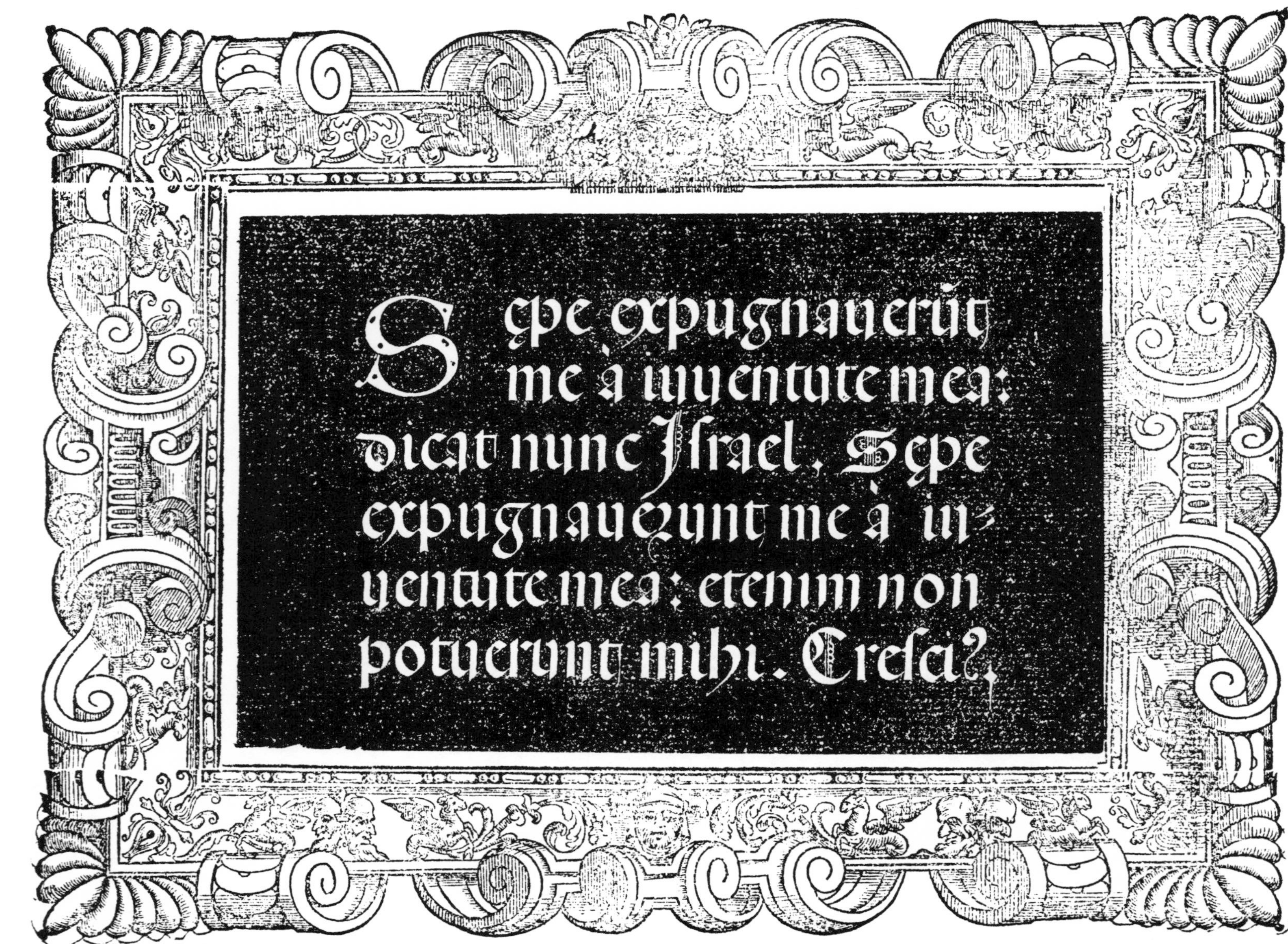
Sępe expugnauerũt
me à iuuentute mea:
dicat nunc Israel. Sępe
expugnauerunt me à iu-
uentute mea: etenim non
potuerunt mihi. Cresci.

Capitall Lrs.

Plate 65: Beauchesne and Baildon, London (?), 1571

Lettere Piaceuolle.

Demostene dice, che a nobili, & honesti huomini in prima si couiene
la beltà del volto, & la moderazione dell'animo: & che queste due
parti hanno bisogno di fortezza: & che l'altre dilicatezze, & lasciuie
hanno grazia nell' herbe, & fiori.

A B C D E F G H I K L M N O P Q R S T V.

PLATE 66: Beauchesne and Baildon, London (?), 1571

Secretarye hande.

Geue not that whiche is holy vnto dogge, neither cast ye
your pearles before swyne, least they treade them vnder
their feete. and the other turne agayne and all to rent you.
Aske and it shalbe geuen yow. seke and ye shall fynd helpe

a b c d e f g h i k l m n o p q r s t u x
y z s st w et.

PLATE 67: Beauchesne and Baildon, London (?), 1571

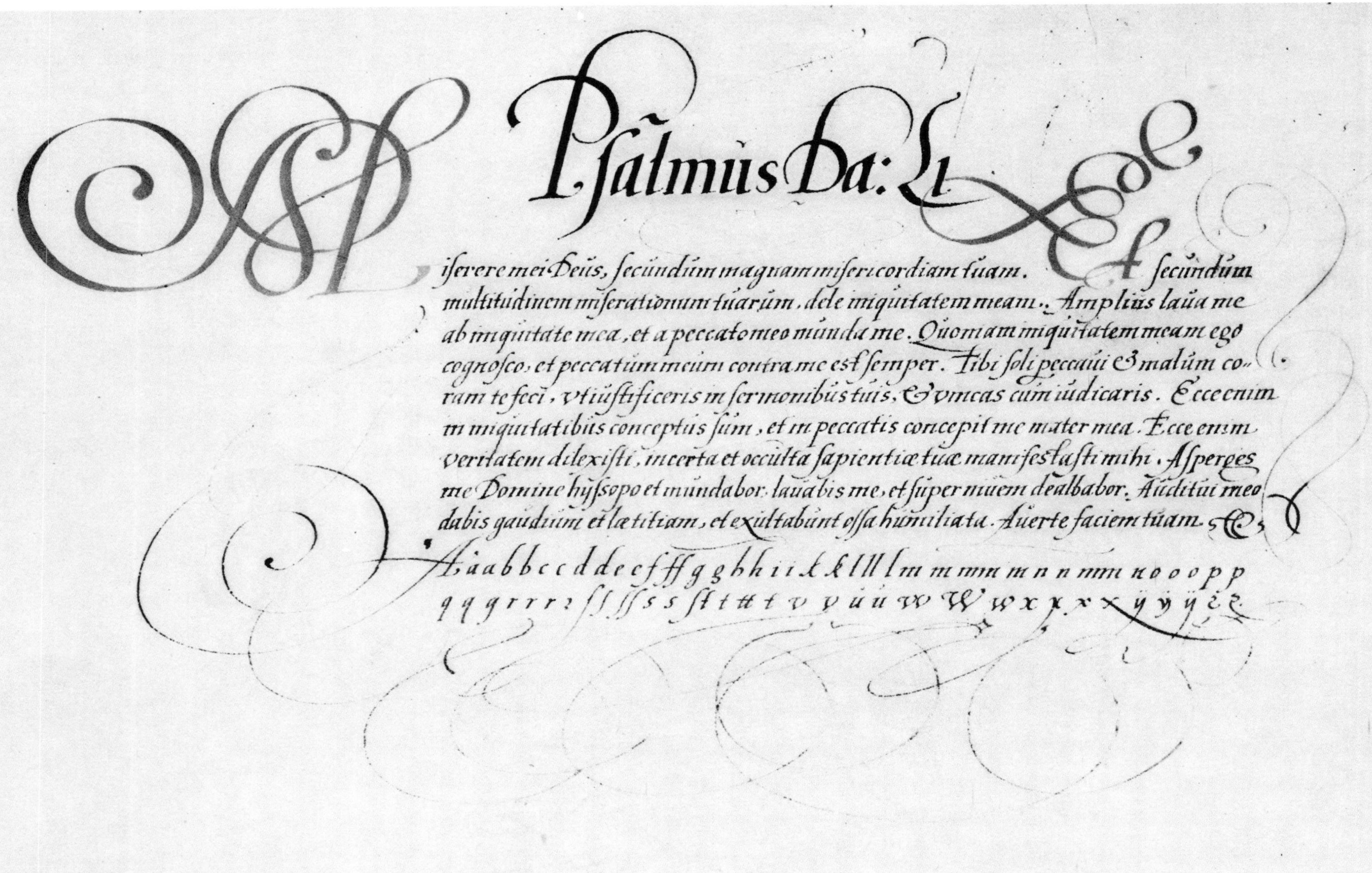

PLATE 68: Leupolt, Markörlbach, 1596

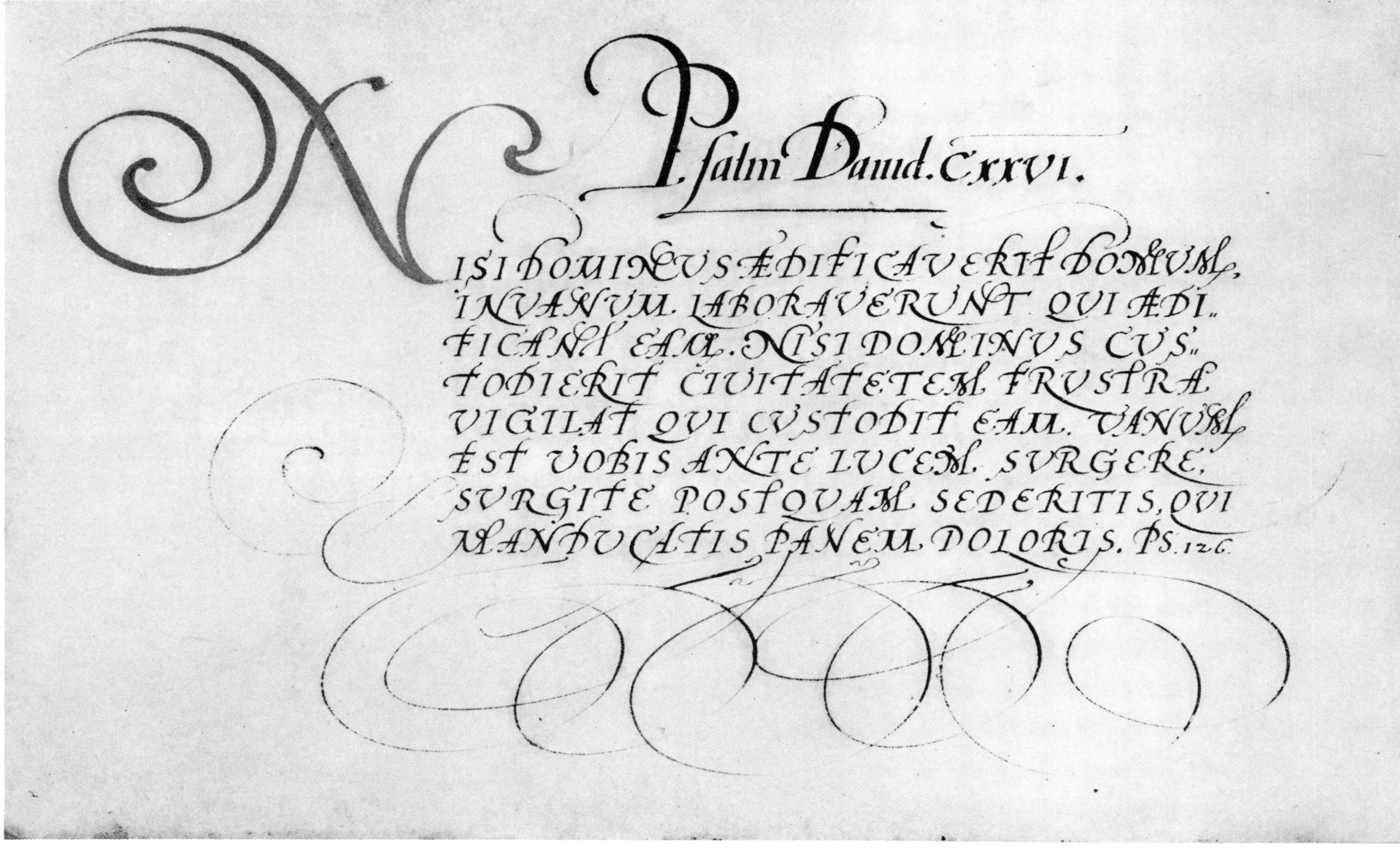

PLATE 69: Leupolt, Markörlbach, 1596

PLATE 79: Leupolt, Markörlbach, 1606

Dem Erbarn vnnd Ehrnthafften Stephan Brechtel, Bürger
vnnd Rechenmaister in München, meinem besonders günstigen lieben Herrn vnd freund
Embeut ich Andreas Gundelfinger Bürger vnnd Rechenmaister zu Nürnberg meinen gantz
willigen vnnd freundlichen dienst, vnnd thu ewer Ehrnthafft hiemit zuuernemmen Nach
dem mir Jeronimus Unger von Augspurg geschrieben vnnd gebetten von wegen der Landlerischen
handlungen halben wie die sachen beschaffen, damit ich wissenschafft haben möge. Dero
wegen gelanngt an euch mein gantz freundlich vnnd vleissig bitten. Dieweil mir
gedachter Jeronimus Unger geschrieben, wollet mir ewer mainung vnnd gutdunckhen was in
dieser sach fürzunemmen zuhandlen vnd zuthun ist das für der lichst Schrifftlich vnd wolmer
wart zuwissen machen. Soll dennach ernennten Ungern von mir alsbald kund gethan

PLATE 71: Leupolt, Markörlbach, 1596

Er straffe mich nicht in deinem zorn und züchtige mich nicht in deinem

PLATE 73: Leupolt, Markörlbach, 1596

PLATE 73: Leupolt, Markörlbach, 1596

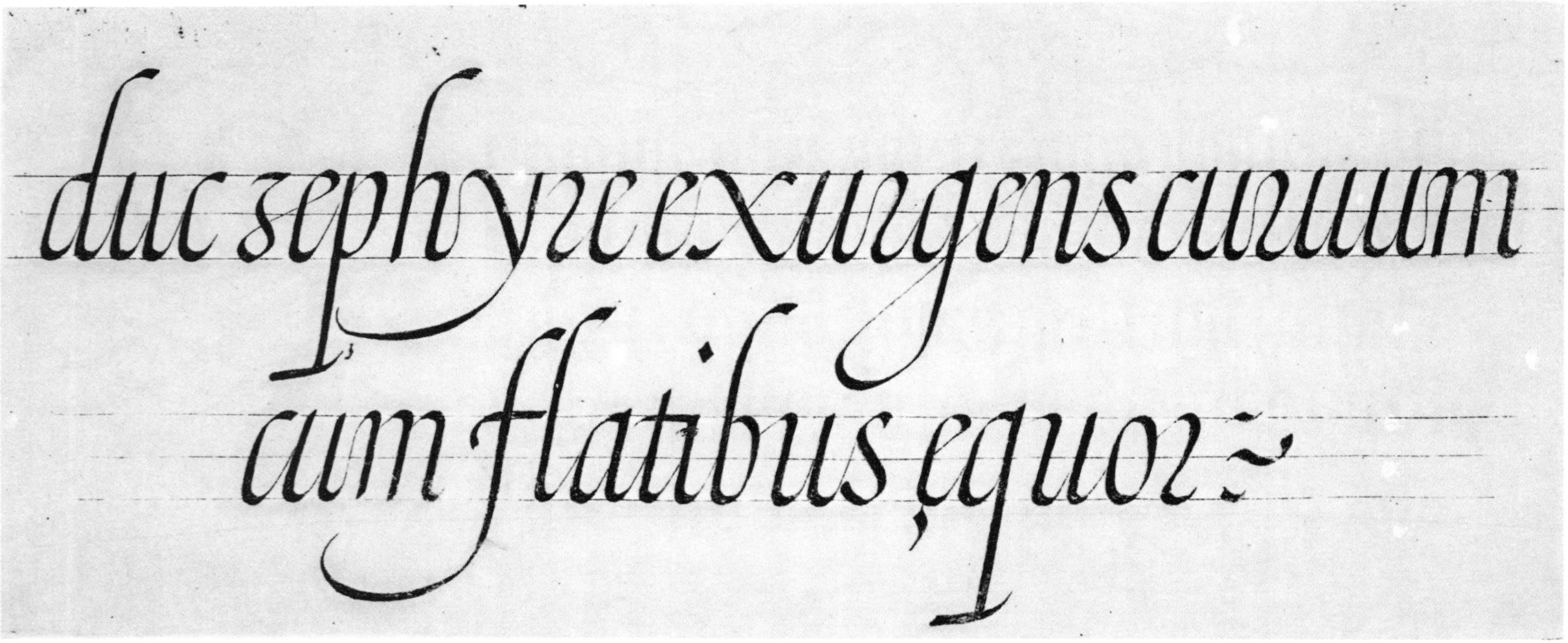

duc zephyre exurgens cur tuum
cum flatibus ęquor

PLATE 74: Morellus, Besançon, 1606

PLATE 75: Morellus, Besançon, 1606

Amicitia plurimas res continet, nunquam
intempestiua, nunquam molesta est: Itaque
nec aqua, nec igni, nec aere (vt aiunt) multis
locis vtimur, vt amicitia, nam et secundas
res meliores facit amicitia. biuhuxinyiszk.
B: Morellus scrib:

PLATE 76: Morellus, Besançon, 1606

H: hore auff von vnmessiger begird zuwissen vnnd zuleernen
dann darinn wirdt vil zerstorung vnnd regierung funden
dann welche vil wissen, die wollen gesehen sein, vnd hören
gern das die woyss gehaissen werden. Es seind vil ding
die der seel zuwissen gar wenig oder nichts nuts seind ~
Kupingimxum.

PLATE 77: Morellus, Besançon, 1606

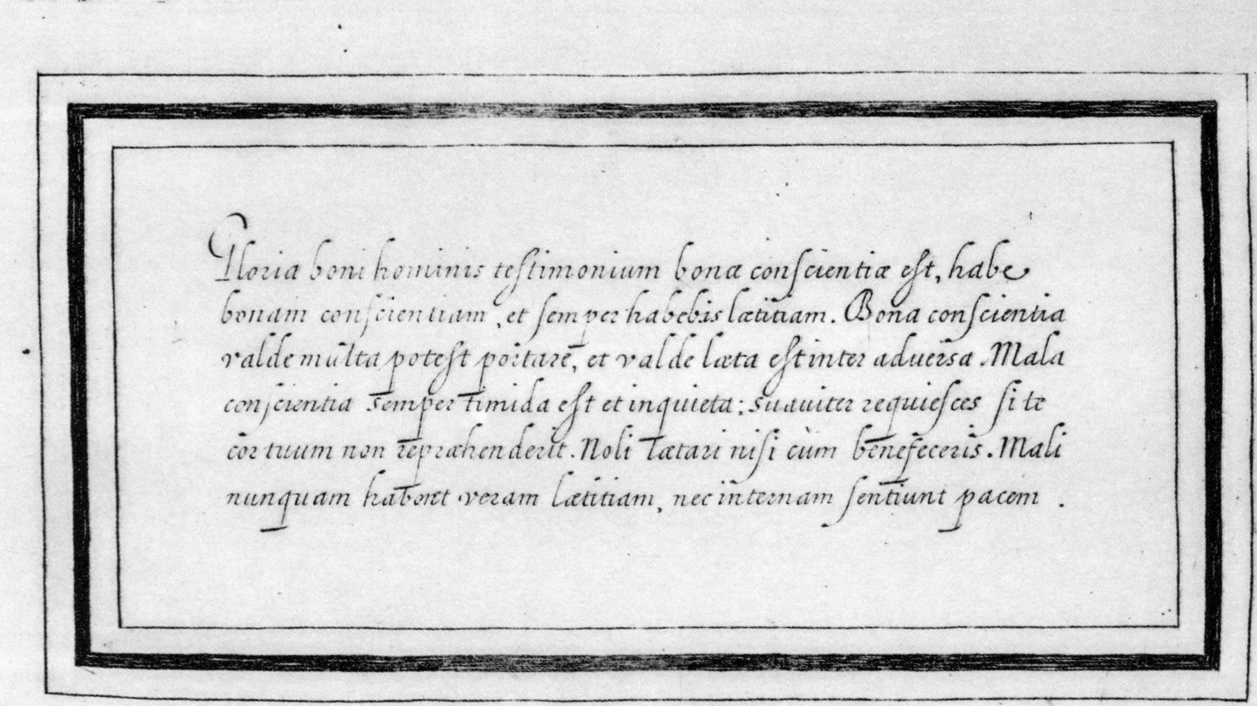

Gloria boni hominis testimonium bonæ conscientiæ est, habe
bonam conscientiam, et semper habebis lætitiam. Bona conscientia
valde multa potest portare, et valde læta est inter aduersa. Mala
conscientia semper timida est et inquieta; suauiter requiesces si te
cor tuum non reprehenderit. Noli lætari nisi cum benefeceris. Mali
nunquam habent veram lætitiam, nec internam sentiunt pacem.

Plate 78: Morellus, Besançon, 1606

Omnes qui alterum in iudicium vocant, preuidere debent non solùm
quid oneris in presentia tollant, sed etiam quantum in omnem vitam
negotij suscipere conentur, legem enim sibi ipsi indicant innocentiæ
continentiæ, virtutumq omnium qui ab altero rationem vitæ reposcunt,
atque eo magis si id faciant nulla re commoti. Nam qui sibi hoc sumpsit
vt mores corrigat aliorum, quis huic ignoscat? Duc Zephyre exurgens
curuum cum flatibus æquor.

Benignus Morellus scribebat.

PLATE 79: Morellus, Besançon, 1606

PLATE 80: van den Velde, Rotterdam, 1605

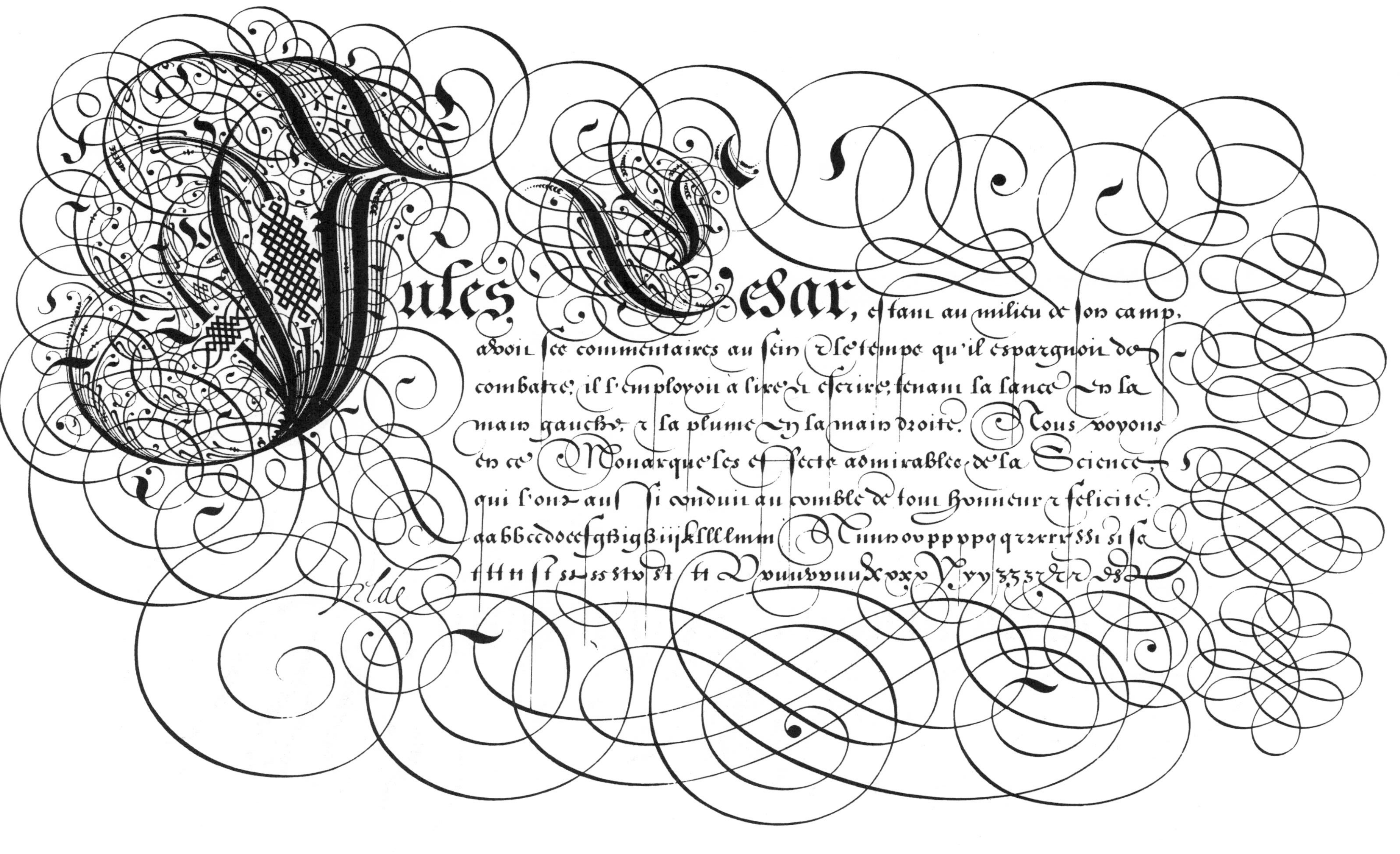

PLATE 81: van den Velde, Rotterdam, 1605

Chilo van Lacedemonien

onder andere syne sententien die meest betrachtens weerdich waren,
sijnde datter gheen schoonder wetenschap en was, dan hem selven te
kennen. Daer naer, datter eynde van allen twist en oneenicheyt
waer iammer ende miserie. Ende ten derden dat een mensche
niet te veel en behoorde te begeeren, maer te vreden te wesen
met genoechsaemheyt. Welcke drije sententien als
Oraclen, dat is, voor Goddelycke antwoorden zijn aengenomen
gheweest, ende inden Tempel tot Delphis met gulden
letteren aengeschreven.

Velde.

PLATE 82: van den Velde, Rotterdam, 1605

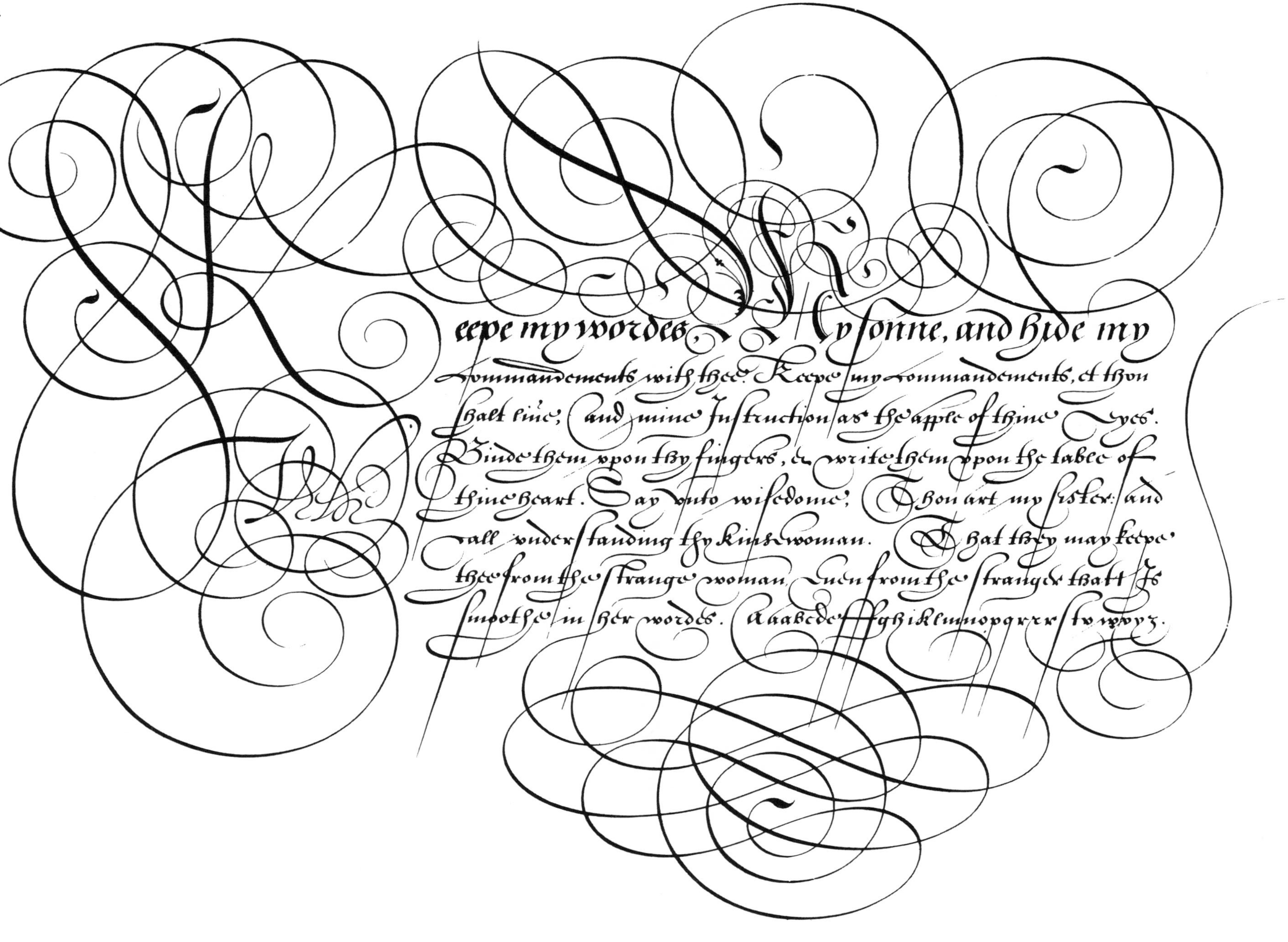

PLATE 83: van den Velde, Rotterdam, 1605

A mon singul. Amy, et tres-cher Comp. Mr.
Nicolas Roo-Claes.

Il n'y a chose plus louable aux hommes que de perseverer fermement en l'amitié
une fois conceuë et fondée sur l'immuable rocher de vertu comme celle
qui ne peut estre esbranlée d'aucun vent de fortune ou de quelque esloignement
de personnes. Certainement celle a esté jusques à present l'amitié de nous
deux. Car nonobstant nre transmigration et longue absence elle s'est
tousjours maintenue ferme et stable entre la mutation du temps et ne
se changera jamais tant que Lachesis daignera filer le fil de nre vie. A Dieu.

Entierement Vre.

Velde

PLATE 84: van den Velde, Rotterdam, 1605

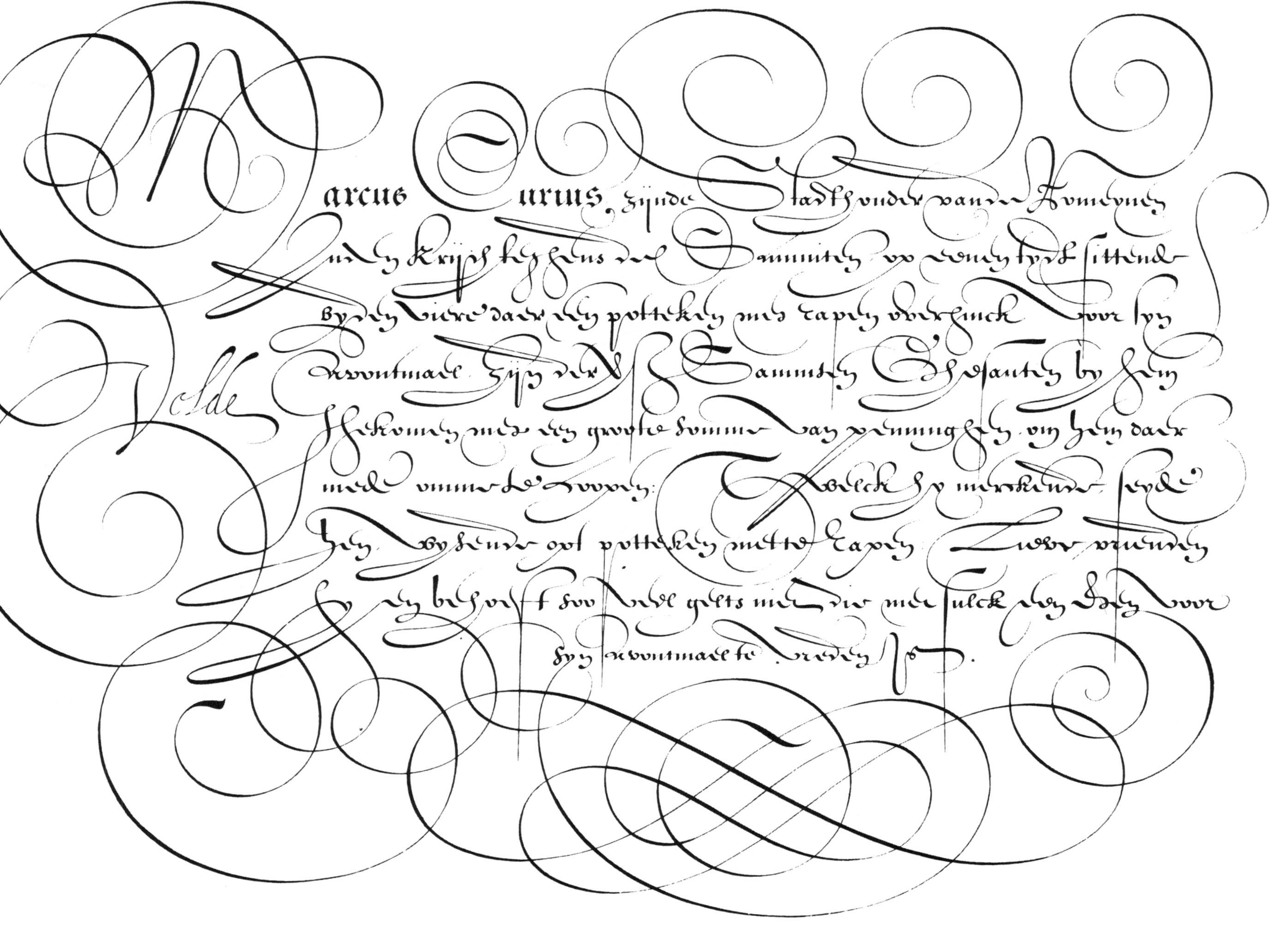

PLATE 85: van den Velde, Rotterdam, 1605

PLATE 86: van den Velde, Rotterdam, 1605

PLATE 87: van den Velde, Rotterdam, 1605

PLATE 88: van den Velde, Rotterdam, 1605

PLATE 89: van den Velde, Rotterdam, 1605

PLATE 90: van den Velde, Rotterdam, 1605

Plate 91: van den Velde, Rotterdam, 1605

A muy Virtuoso Prudente y Discreto S.r Gaspar
Hoermans, Mercader en Rotterdamo.

Como p diuersas vezes he experimentado la mucha afecion q V. M.
tiene a la Letra de qualquiera buen Escriuano, No he podido dexar de
offrecerle esta Letra Espangnola. Pues ay dias q se entendido los negocios
que V.M. y la dicha Nacion Espangnola tiene, y En el credito
que para con ellos V.M. me podra poner: he tomado el atreuimiento de
importunar a V.M. destos pocos renglones. Suplicando le me mande
en lo q le conuiniere de su seruicio. Y con tanto a Dios os encomiendo. &c.

Velde

PLATE 92: van den Velde, Rotterdam, 1605

PLATE 93: van den Velde, Rotterdam, 1605

PLATE 94: van den Velde, Rotterdam, 1605

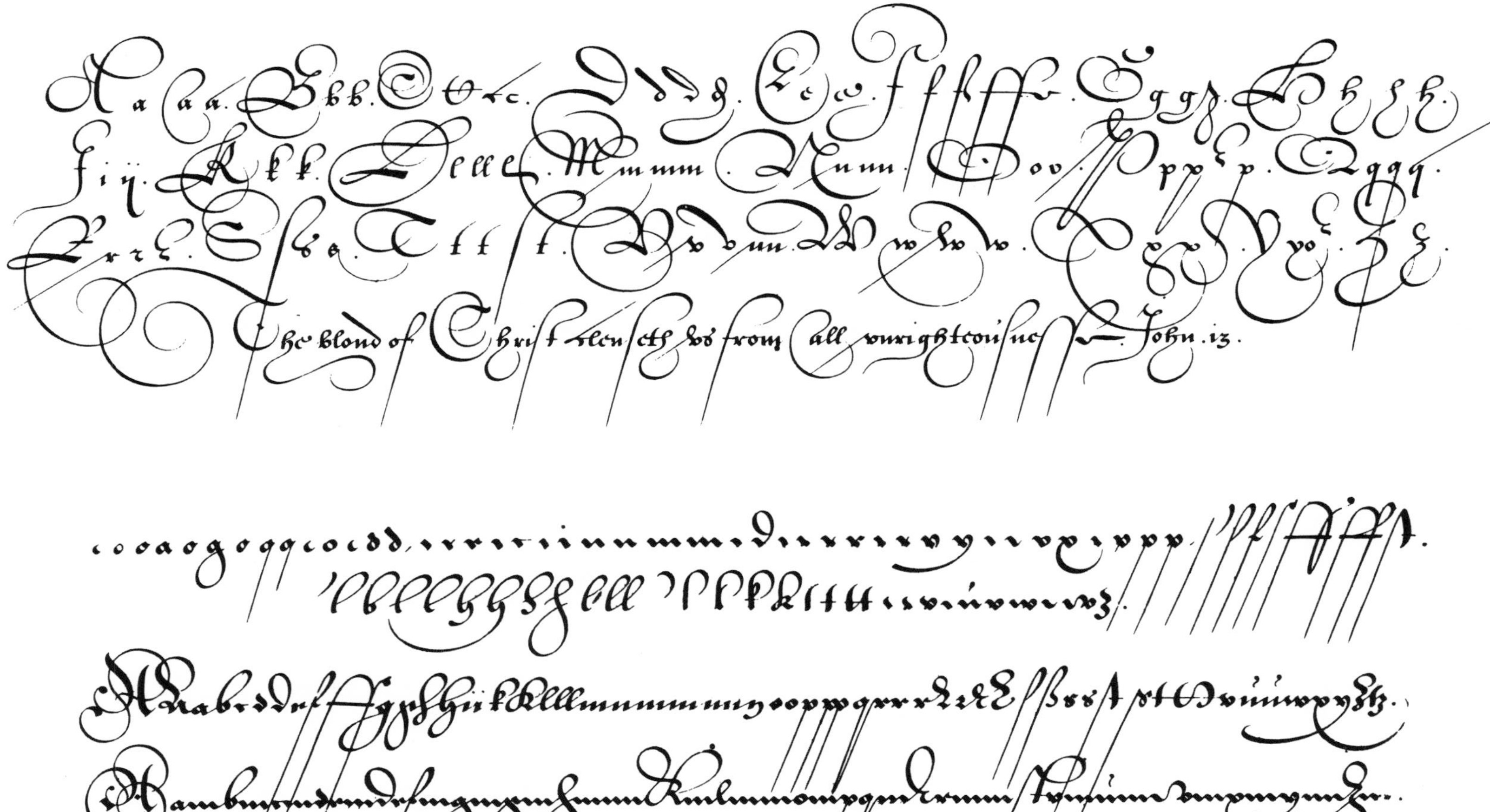

PLATE 95: van den Velde, Rotterdam, 1605

PLATE 96: Rütlinger, Zurich, 1615

PLATE 97: Rütlinger, Zurich, 1615

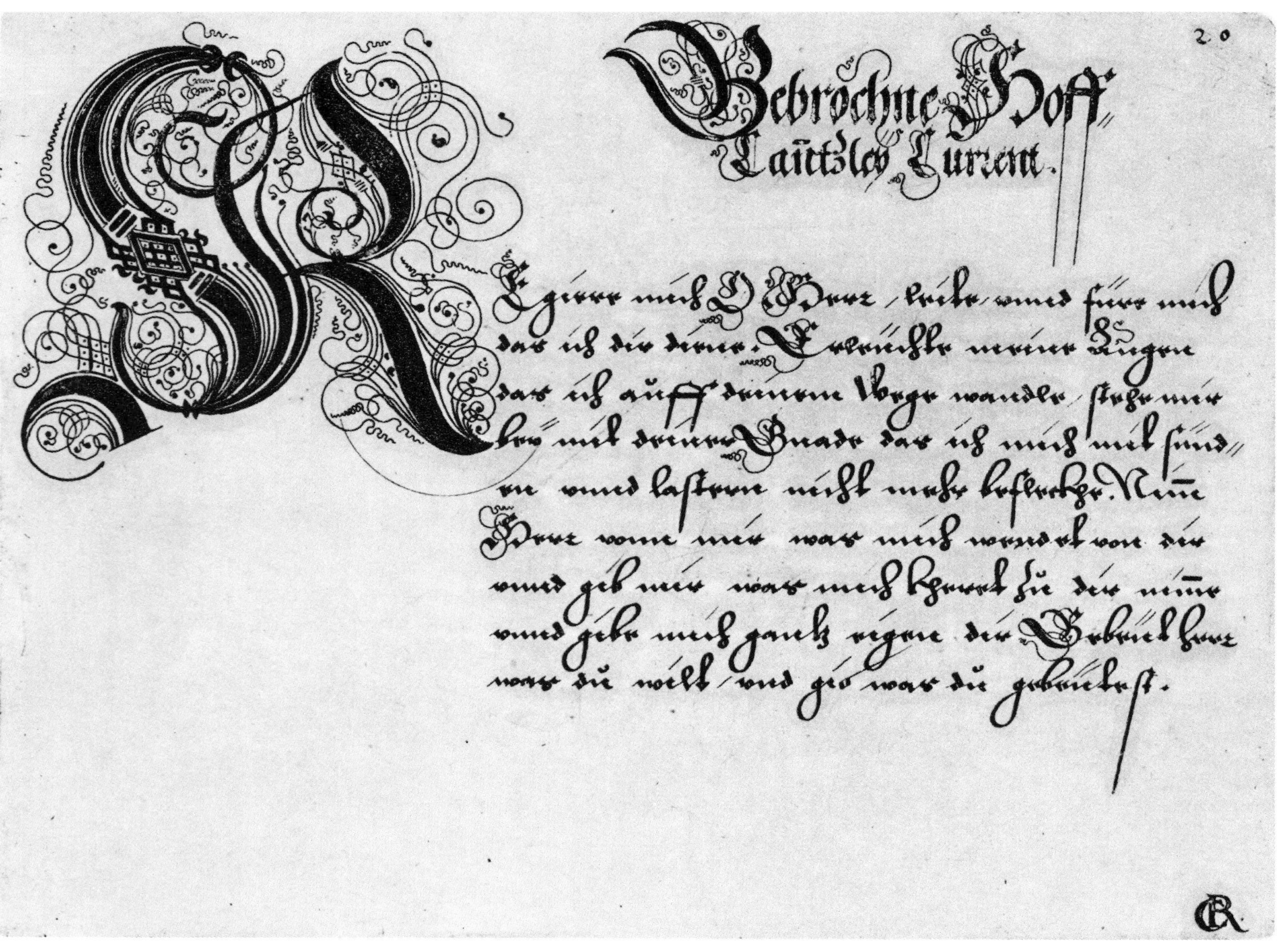

PLATE 98: Rütlinger, Zurich, 1615

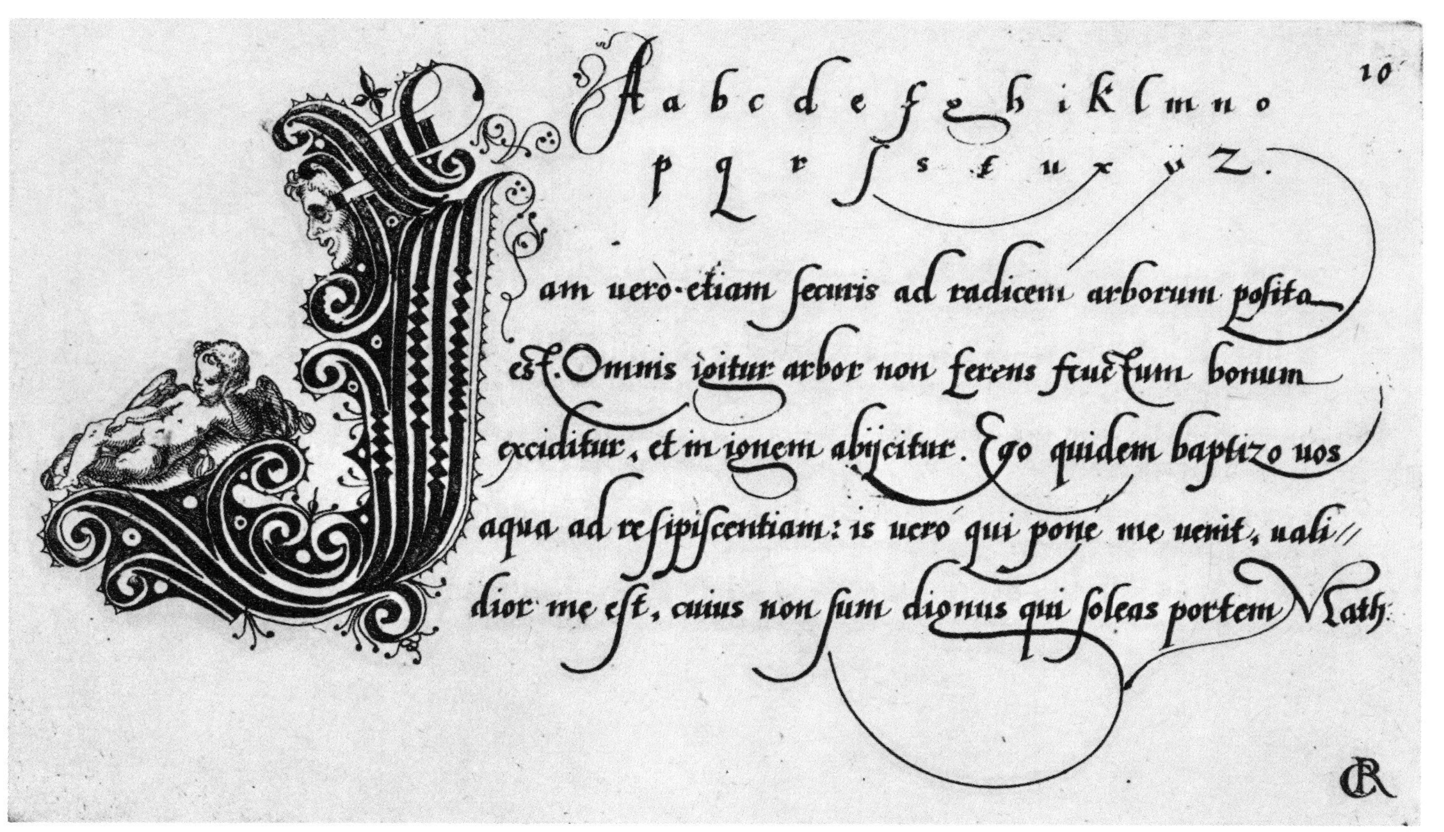

PLATE 99: Rütlinger, Zurich, 1615

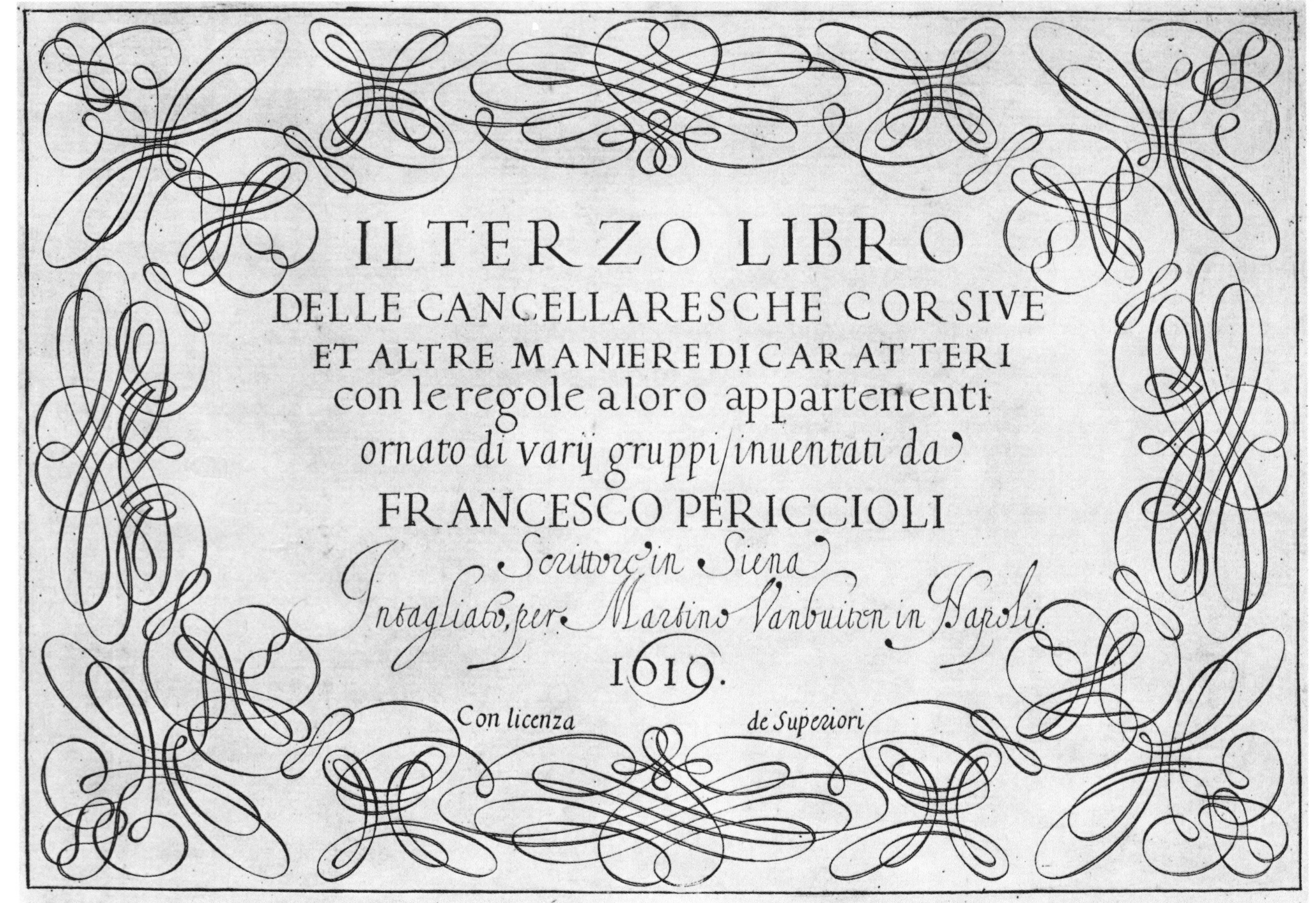

PLATE 100: Periccioli, Siena, 1619

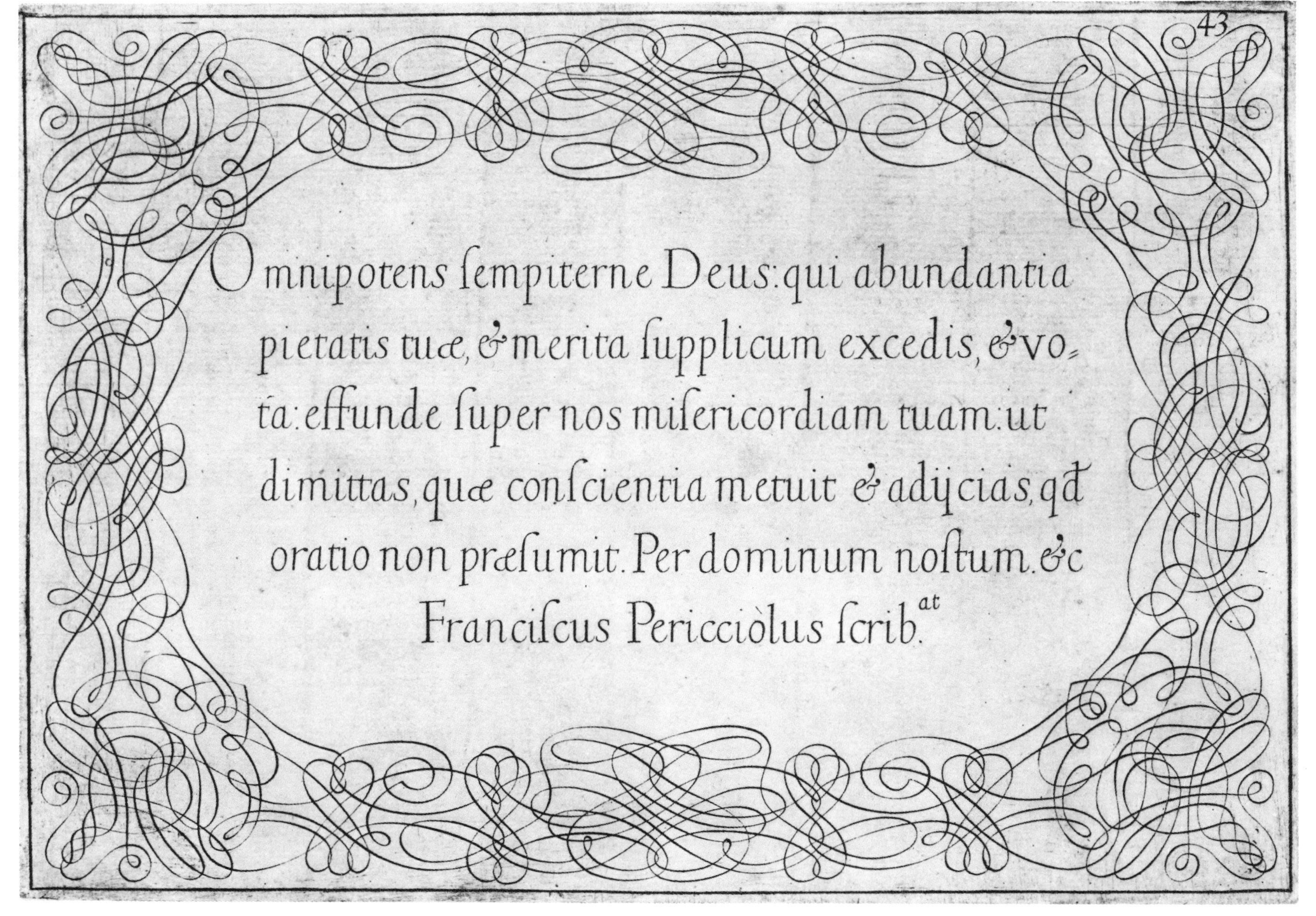

43
Omnipotens sempiterne Deus: qui abundantia
pietatis tuæ, & merita supplicum excedis, & vo-
ta: effunde super nos misericordiam tuam: ut
dimittas, quæ conscientia metuit & adycias, qd
oratio non præsumit. Per dominum nostum. &c
Franciscus Pericciolus scrib.at

PLATE 101: Periccioli, Siena, 1619

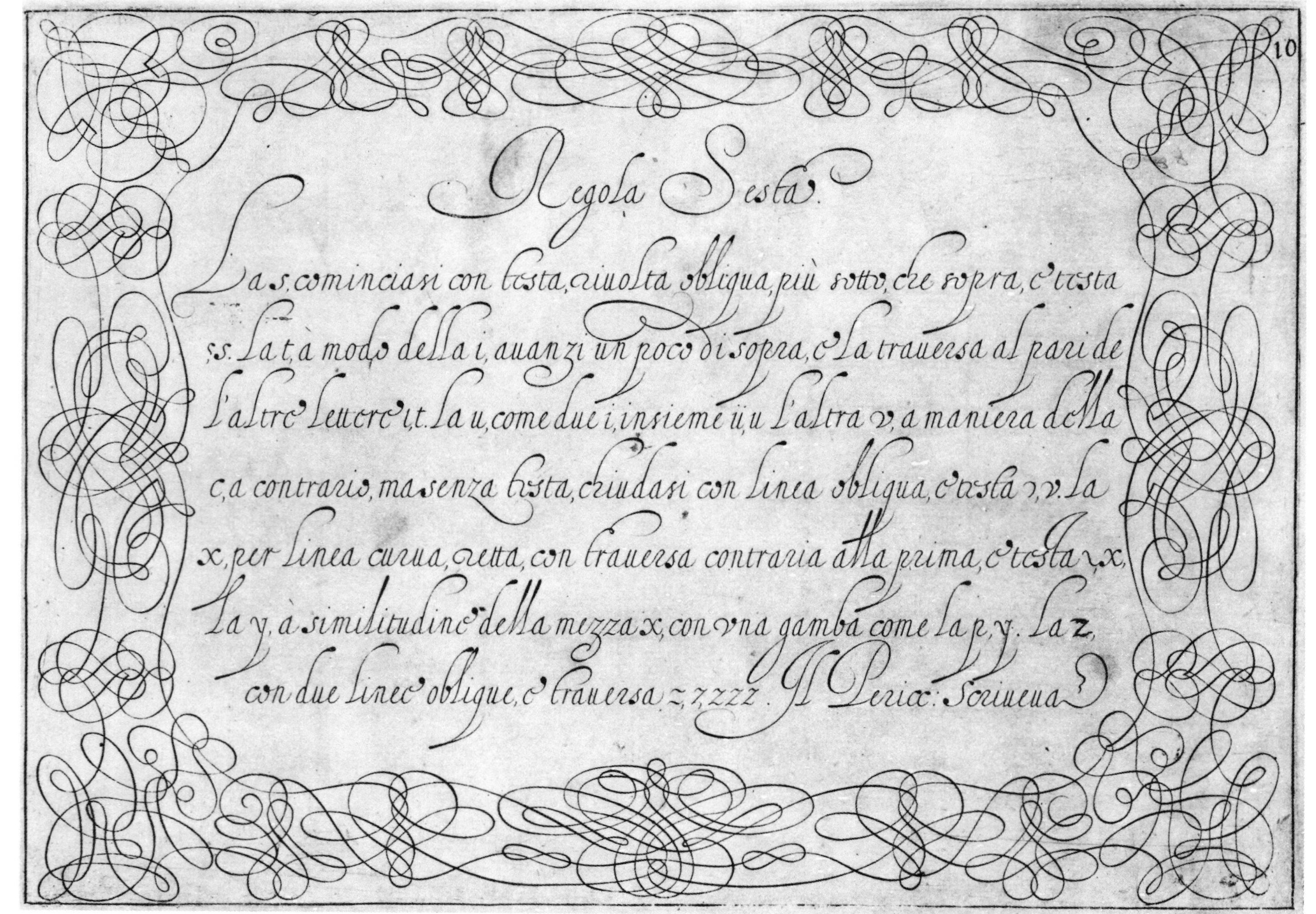

Plate 102: Pericciolі, Siena, 1619

PLATE 103: Periccioli, Siena, 1619

ALPHABET DE LA LRE DOUBLE

ALPHABET DEMONSTANT LA FORME ET PROPORTION

DES LETTRES FINANCIERES RONDES

PLATE 104: Desmoulins, Lyons, 1625

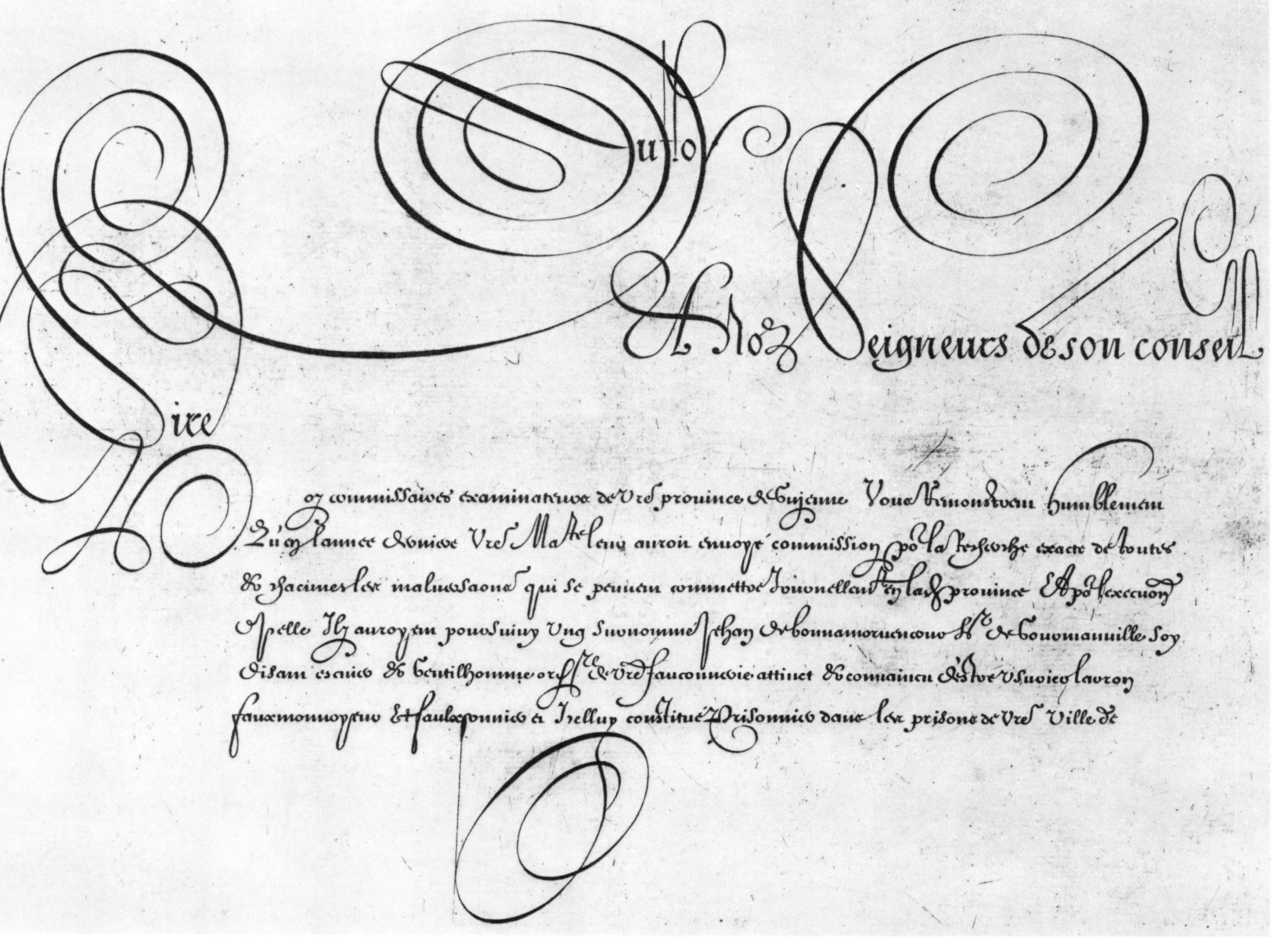

PLATE 105: Desmoulins, Lyons, 1625

PLATE 106: Desmoulins, Lyons, 1625

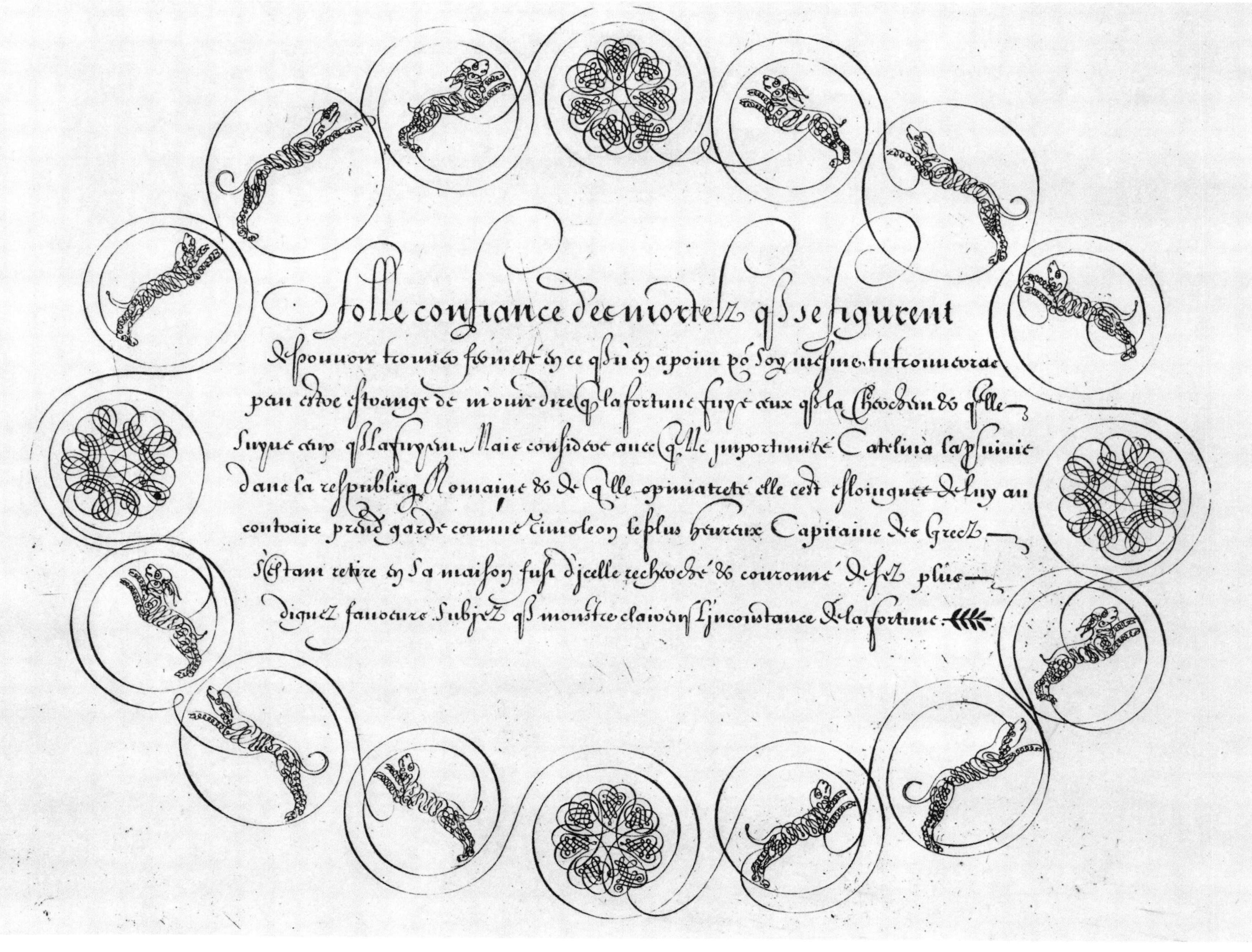

PLATE 107: Desmoulins, Lyons, 1625

PLATE 108: Desmoulins, Lyons, 1625

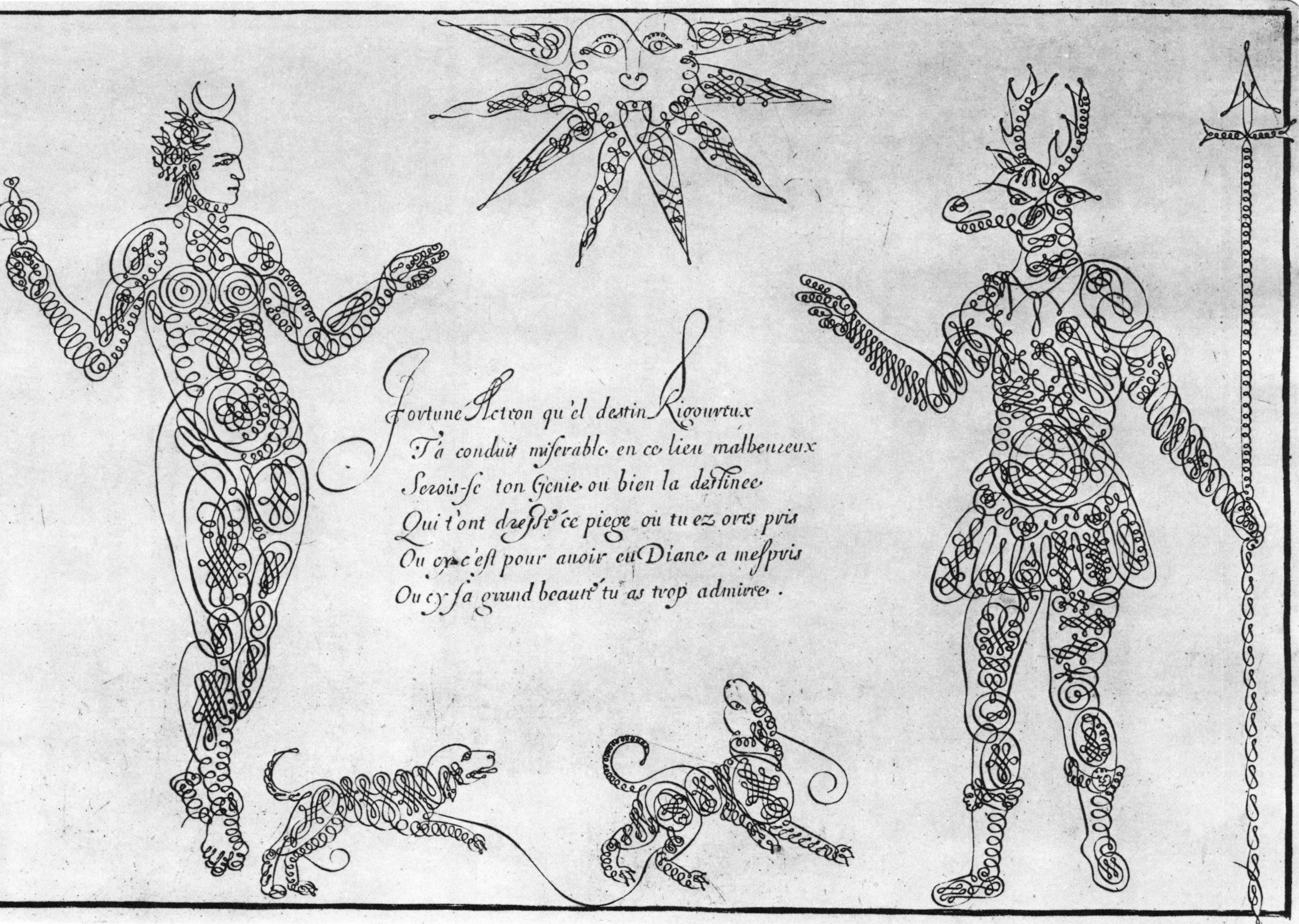

Fortune Acteon qu'el destin Rigoureux
T'a conduit miserable en ce lieu malheureux
Serois-se ton Genie ou bien la destinee
Qui t'ont dressé ce piege ou tu ez ores pris
Ou cy c'est pour auoir eu Diane a mespris
Ou cy sa grand beauté tu as trop admiree .

PLATE 109: Desmoulins, Lyons, 1625

PLATE 110: Desmoulins, Lyons, 1625

PLATE III: Desmoulins, Lyons, 1625

Le pt trompte de la compnie du C. de St Maurice ayt esté envoyé por repetir quelques
prisonnrs lesqls furent pris a franquevaux Nous luy avons donné ce passeport por aller
au bourg de St Martin seulemt por la repetion desd. prisonnrs pourquoy Nous enioignons
& commandons a tous ceux sur lesqls sestend nre pouvoir & commandement & prions tous
autres quil appartiendra de laisser passer & repasser avec toute seureté & liberté
Iceluy pnt trompette marchant & se fiant sur la foy publique sans permettre quil luy soit
fait ou donné aucun empeschement en quelque sorte & maniere que ce soit. En foy de quoy
nous avons signé ce pnt nre passeport a Paris le vingt-cinqme Aoust 1647. xlvij

Barbedor pingebat

PLATE 112: Barbedor. Paris, ca. 1647

PLATE 113: Barbedor, Paris, ca. 1647

Barbedor

PLATE 114: Barbedor, Paris, ca. 1647

Il n'y a chose au monde si facile que de reprendre les ouura-
ges d'autruy: mais en fe: sur semblable subiet qui soient
meilleurs et plus accomplis, c'est ce qui est tres-difficile.
Comme dit vn Lacedemonien quand il oüit dire, que
Philippes Roy de Macedoine auoit fait demolir et razer
la ville d'Olynthe: Mais il n'en sçauroit (dit-il) faire vne telle.
Barbedor

PLATE 115: Barbedor, Paris, ca. 1647

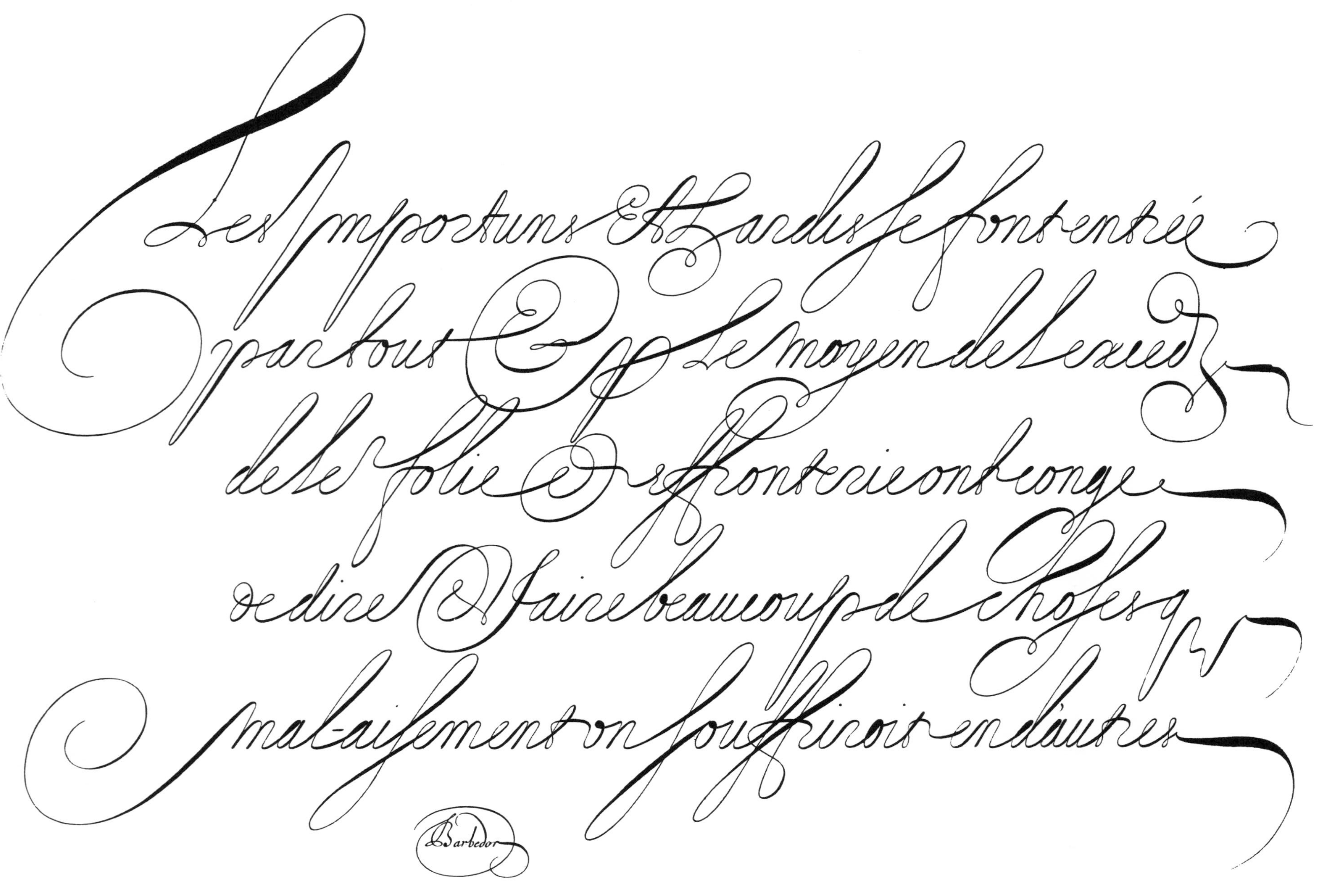

PLATE 116: Barbedor, Paris, ca. 1647

PLATE 117: Senault, Paris, ca. 1670

36

Por quanto el Rey mi señor, y Padre que santa gloria aya, teniendo consideracion a los muchos, y buenos servicios que Antonio Garcia Altamirano le havia hecho en el Officio de Contador de resultas, y en la Contaduria mayor de Cuentas de Contador ordenador della, por una su carta y provision de veinte y tres de Abril de mil y seiscientos y siete, le hizo merced del Officio de Contador de la Santa Cruzada del Tribunal de la ciudad de Mexico: Y despues atendiendo a las grandes utilidades que resultaron a mi Real hacienda, de la inteligencia, y zelo con que sirvio el dicho officio en el discurso de veinte y tres años, por una mi carta y provision de primero de Março del año passado de mil y seiscientos y treinta, hize merced del dicho officio a vos Manuel Garcia Altamirano para despues de los dias del dicho Antonio Garcia Altamirano vuestro padre: y haviendo entrado a servirle por su fallecimiento, pretendio el Fiscal de mi Real Audiencia, y del dicho Tribunal que os havia de preceder en las juntas, y demas actos que hiciese el dicho Tribunal: sobre lo qual se proveyeron algunos autos, y despues de haverse visto en el mi Consejo de la Santa Cru=zada: Por otra mi carta mande se guardase la costumbre que siempre havia havido en el dicho Tribunal, y que en su conformidad precediesedes vos al dicho Fiscal, y a todos los que le sucedieren en el dicho officio, como mas largamente se contiene en los dichos Titulos, y cedula referida y en las condiciones, y declaraciones con que se libraron y despacharon a que me refiero.

PLATE 118: Casanova, Madrid, 1650

28

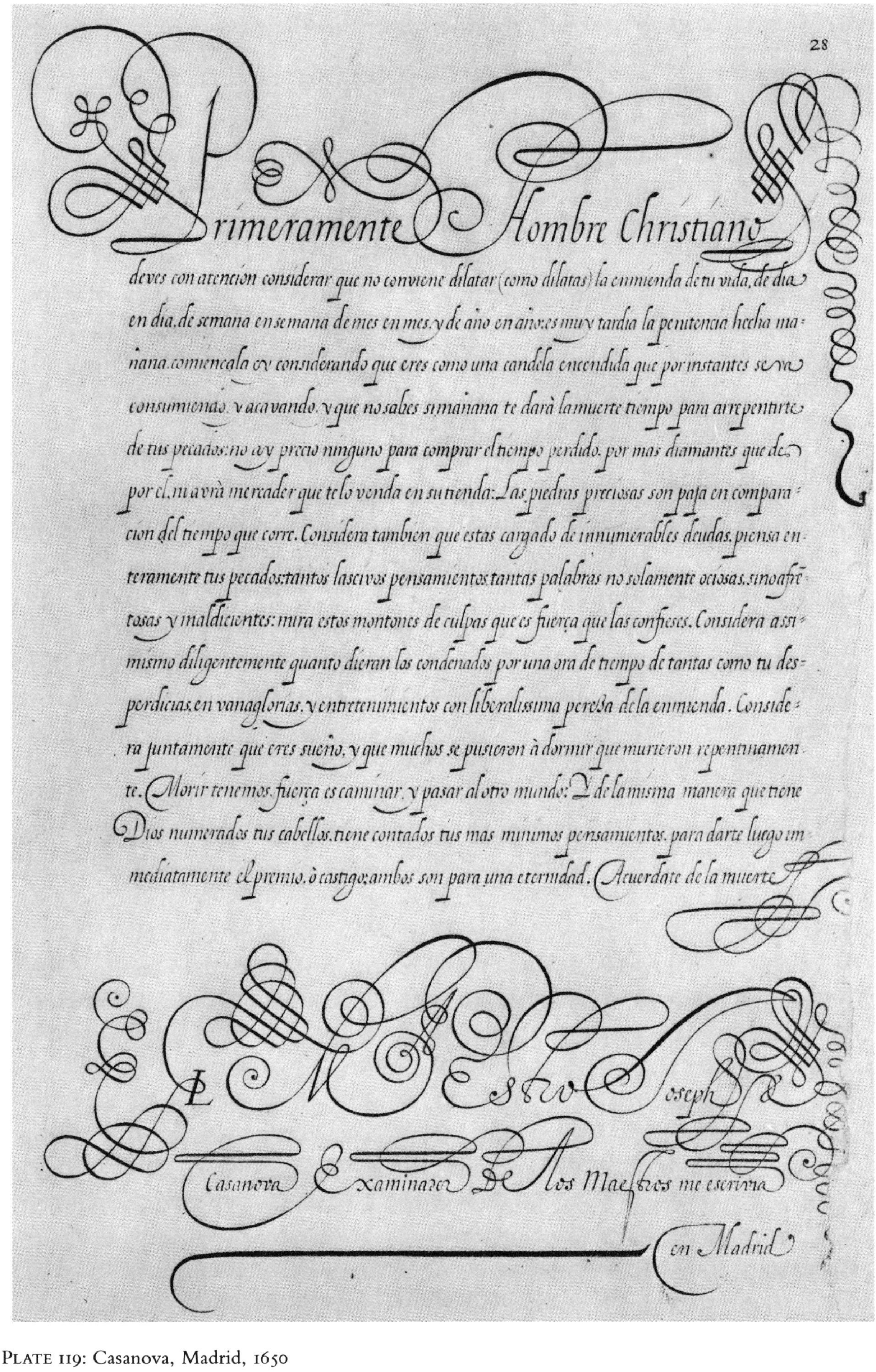

Primeramente Hombre Christiano

deves con atencion considerar que no conviene dilatar (como dilatas) la enmienda de tu vida, de dia en dia, de semana en semana de mes en mes, y de año en año: es muy tardia la penitencia hecha mañana. comiençala oy considerando que eres como una candela encendida que por instantes se va consumiendo, y acavando. y que no sabes si mañana te darà la muerte tiempo para arrepentirte de tus pecados: no ay precio ninguno para comprar el tiempo perdido. por mas diamantes que des por el, ni avrà mercader que te lo venda en su tienda: Las piedras preciosas son paja en comparacion del tiempo que corre. Considera tambien que estas cargado de innumerables deudas, piensa enteramente tus pecados: tantos lascivos pensamientos, tantas palabras no solamente ociosas, sino afrentosas y maldicientes: mira estos montones de culpas que es fuerça que las confieses. Considera assimismo diligentemente quanto dieran los condenados por una ora de tiempo de tantas como tu desperdicias, en vanaglorias, y entretenimientos con liberalissima pereza de la enmienda. Considera juntamente que eres sueño, y que muchos se pusieron à dormir que murieron repentinamente. Morir tenemos, fuerça es caminar, y pasar al otro mundo: Y de la misma manera que tiene Dios numerados tus cabellos, tiene contados tus mas minimos pensamientos, para darte luego inmediatamente el premio, ò castigo: ambos son para una eternidad. Acuerdate de la muerte

El Maestro Joseph de Casanova Examinador de los Maestros me escrivia en Madrid

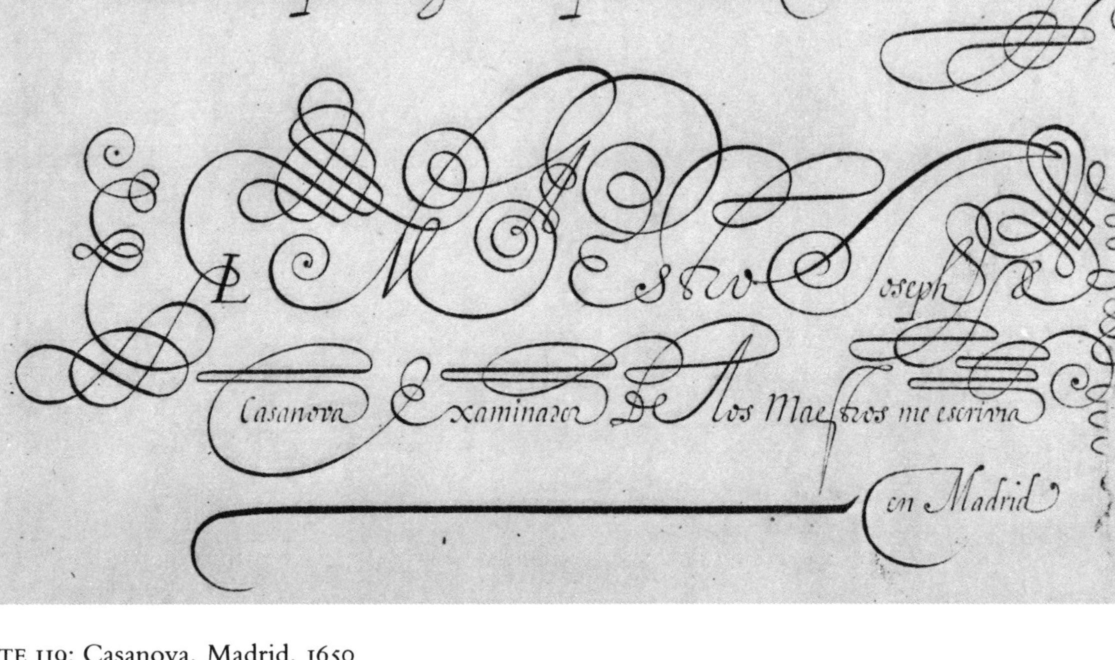

PLATE 119: Casanova, Madrid, 1650

Domine Iesu Christe. Fili Dei vivi, pone passiònem, Crucem, & mortē tuam inter iudicium tuum & ánimam meam, nunc, & in hora mortis meæ: & mihi largiri dignêris grátiam, & misericordiam, vivis & defunctis requiem, & veniam, Ecclésiæ tuæ pacem & concordiam, & nobis peccatoribus vitam & gloriam sempiternam. Qui vivis & regnas cum Deo Patre. Etta.

Deus indulgentiârum Dómine: da animâbus famulôrum famularúmque tuârum, quorum anniversáriū depositionis diē commemorâmus: refrigérij sedem, quiètis beatitúdinem & lúminis claritatem. Per Dóminum nostrum Iesum Christum Filium tuum; qui tecum vivit & regnat in unitate Spiritus Sancti Deus. per omnia. &a.

EN LA INSIGNE VILLA DE MADRID ME ESCRIVIA EL MAESTRO
IOSEPH DE CASANOVA EXAMINADOR DE LOS MAESTROS DE SV
ARTE VIVIENDO EN LA PVERTA DE GVADALAIARA DONDE RECIBE
PVPILOS E YGVALADOS. ESCRIVE EXECVTORIAS Y PRIVILEGIOS

PLATE 120: Casanova, Madrid, 1650

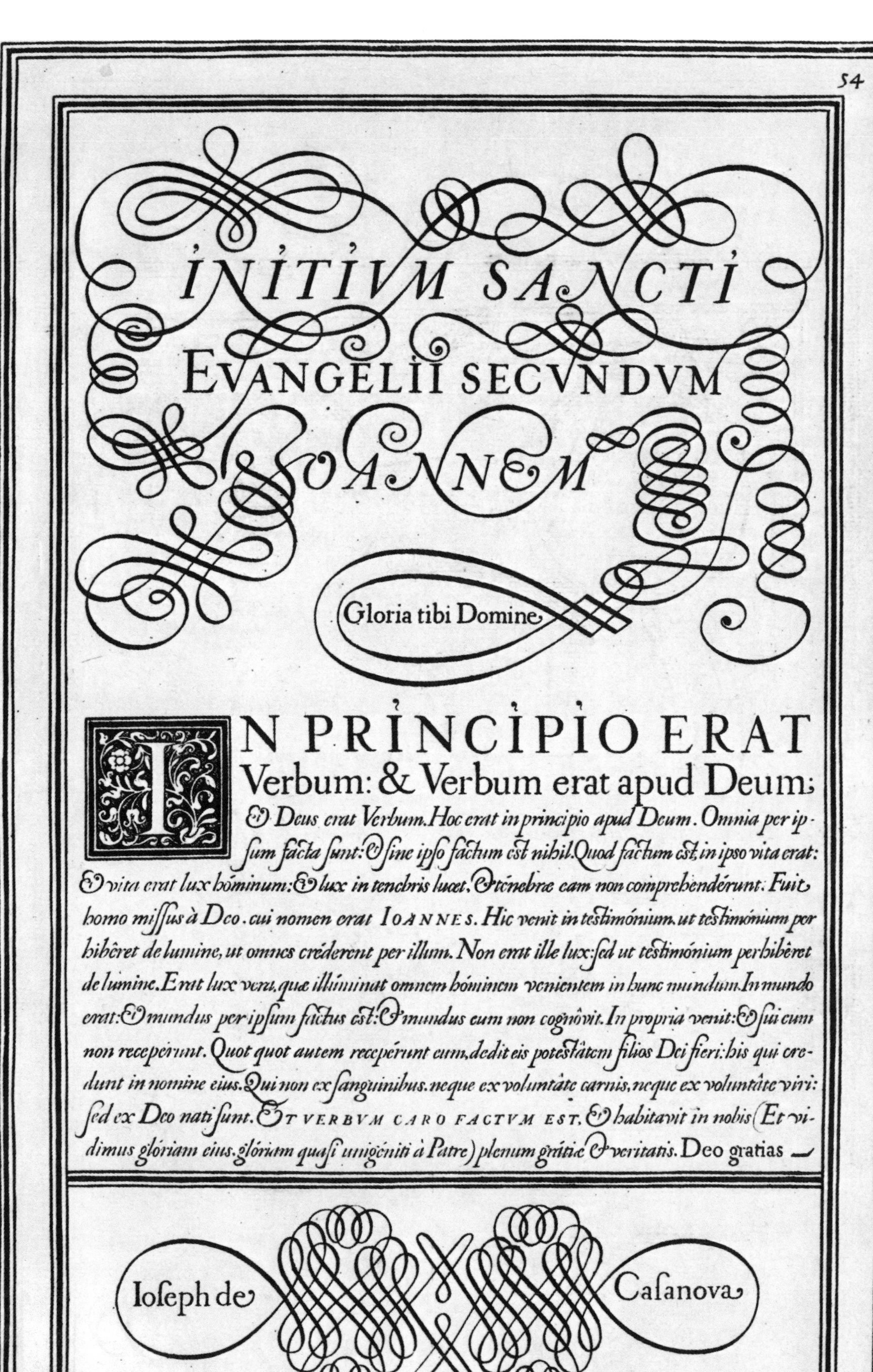

54

INITIVM SANCTI EVANGELII SECVNDVM IOANNEM

Gloria tibi Domine

IN PRINCIPIO ERAT Verbum: & Verbum erat apud Deum; & Deus erat Verbum. Hoc erat in principio apud Deum. Omnia per ipsum facta sunt: & sine ipso factum est nihil. Quod factum est, in ipso vita erat: & vita erat lux hóminum: & lux in tenebris lucet. & ténebræ eam non comprehendérunt. Fuit homo missus à Deo. cui nomen erat IOANNES. Hic venit in testimónium, ut testimónium perhibêret de lumine, ut omnes créderent per illum. Non erat ille lux: sed ut testimónium perhibêret de lumine. Erat lux vera, quæ illúminat omnem hóminem venientem in hunc mundum. In mundo erat: & mundus per ipsum factus est: & mundus eum non cognôvit. In propria venit: & sui eum non recepérunt. Quot quot autem recepérunt eum, dedit eis potestâtem filios Dei fieri: his qui credunt in nomine eius. Qui non ex sanguinibus, neque ex voluntâte carnis, neque ex voluntâte viri: sed ex Deo nati sunt. ET VERBVM CARO FACTVM EST. & habitavit in nobis (Et vidimus glóriam eius, glóriam quasi unigéniti à Patre) plenum grâtiæ & veritatis. Deo gratias

Ioseph de Casanova

PLATE 121: Casanova, Madrid, 1650

Wie wirt ein Jüngling seinen Weg unsträfflich gehen? Wenn er sich helt nach deinen Worten. Ich suche dich von gantzem hertzen, lass mich nicht fehlen deiner Gebott. Ich behalt dein Wort in meinem hertzen, auff dass ich nicht wider dich sündige. Gelobet seystu Herr, lehre mich deine Rechte. Ich wil mit meinen lippen erzehlen alle Rechte deines mundts. Ich freue mich des wegs deiner zeugnuss, als über allerley reichthumb. Ich rede, was du befohlen hast, unnd schawe auff deine Wege. Ich habe lust zu deinen Rechten, und vergesse deiner Worten nit. Thu wol deinem Knecht, dass ich lebe, und dein Wort halte. Öffne mir die augen, dass ich sehe die wunder an deinem Gesatz. Ich bin ein gast auff Erden, verbirg deine Gebott nit für mir. Meine Seele ist zumalmet für verlangen nach deinen Rechten allezeit. Spricht der heilige Prophet David im 119 Psalm.

PLATE 122: Hochreutiner, St. Gallen, 1658

PLATE 123: Hochreutiner, St. Gallen, 1658

PLATE 124: Senault, Paris, ca. 1670

PLATE 125: Senault, Paris, ca. 1670

PLATE 126: Petré, Paris, ca. 1670

PLATE 127: Petré, Paris, ca. 1670

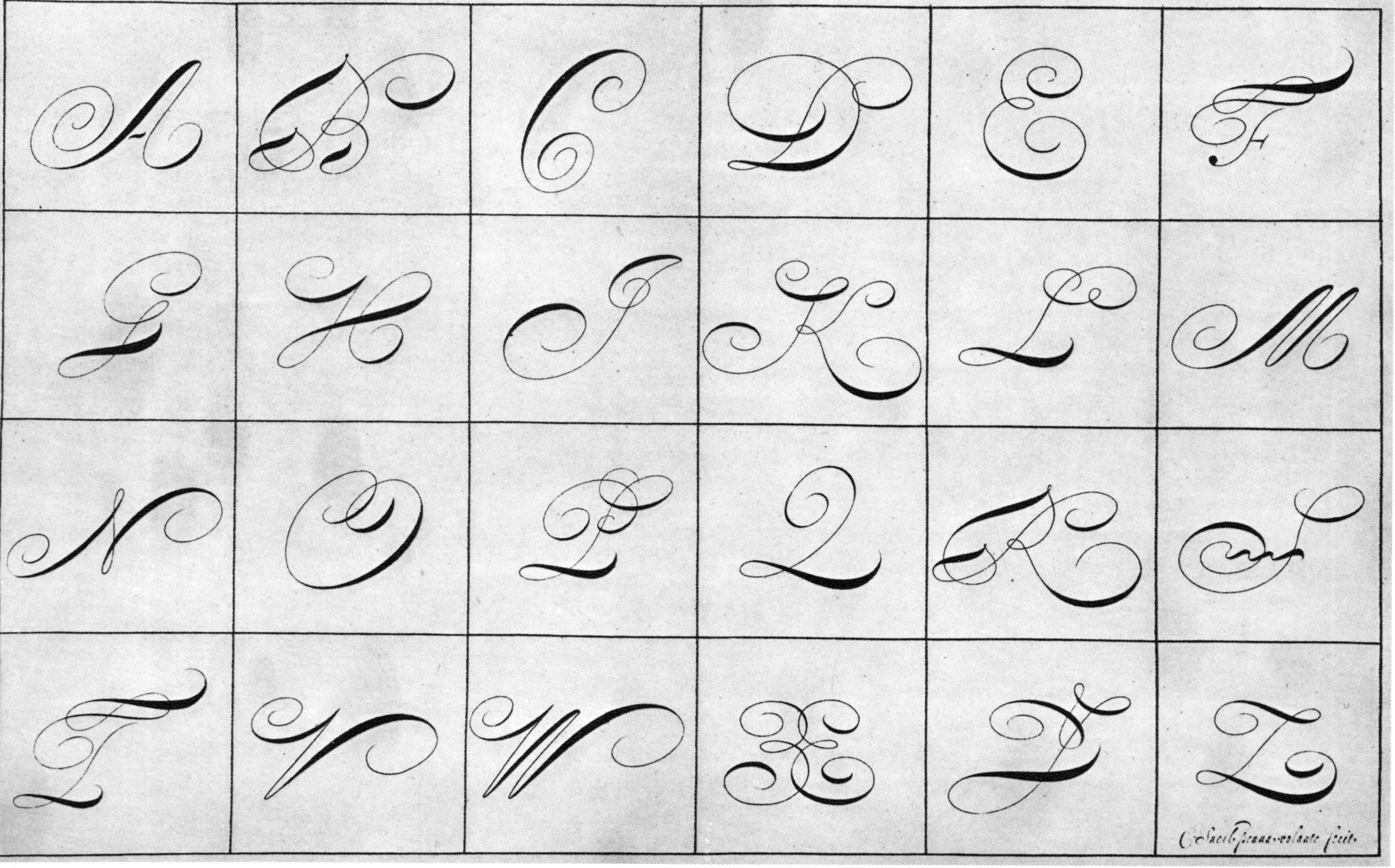

PLATE 128: Snell, London, 1694 and 1714

PLATE 129: Snell, London, 1694 and 1714

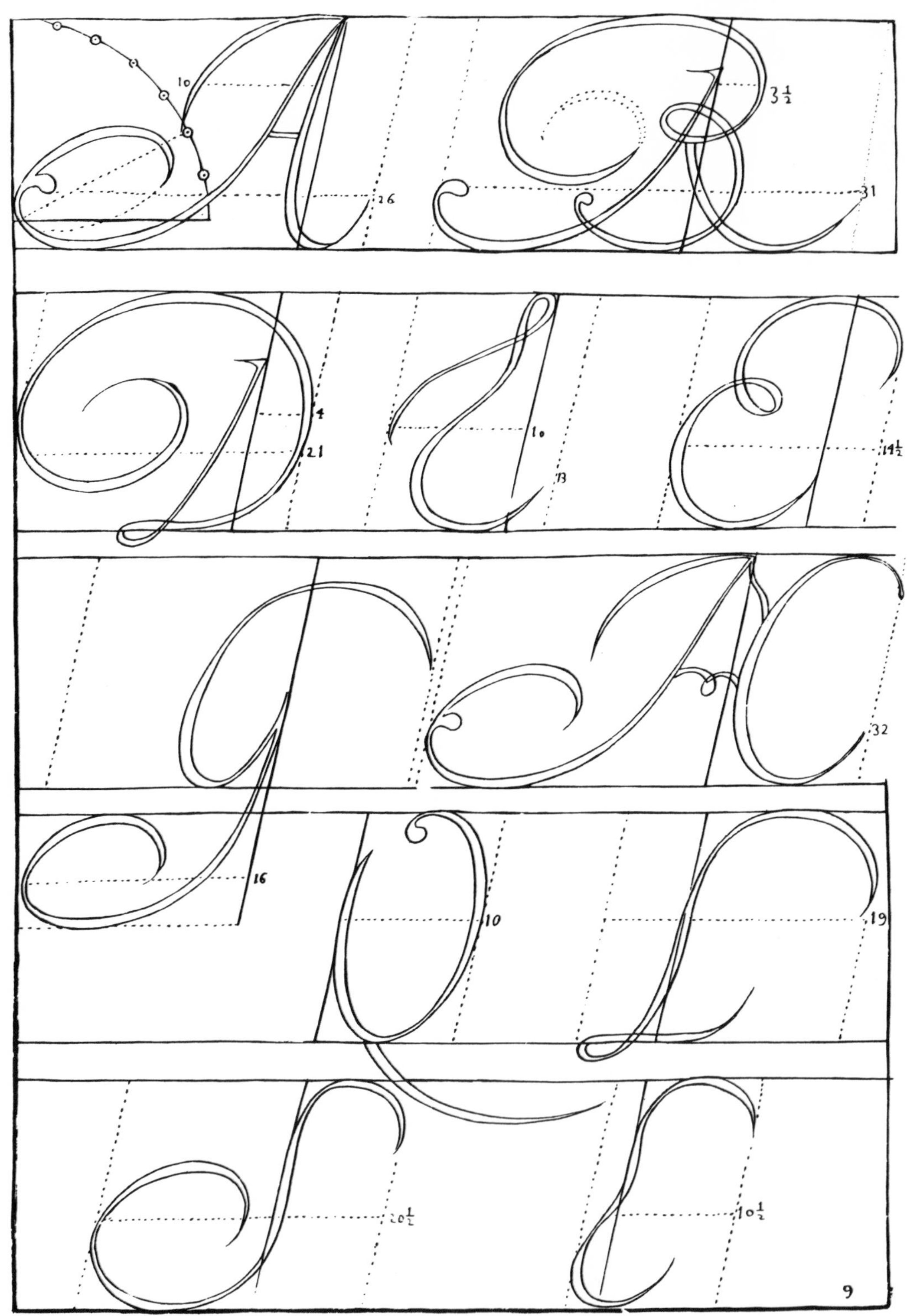

PLATE 130: Polanco, Madrid, 1719

PLATE 131: Polanco, Madrid, 1719

PLATE 132: Polanco, Madrid, 1719

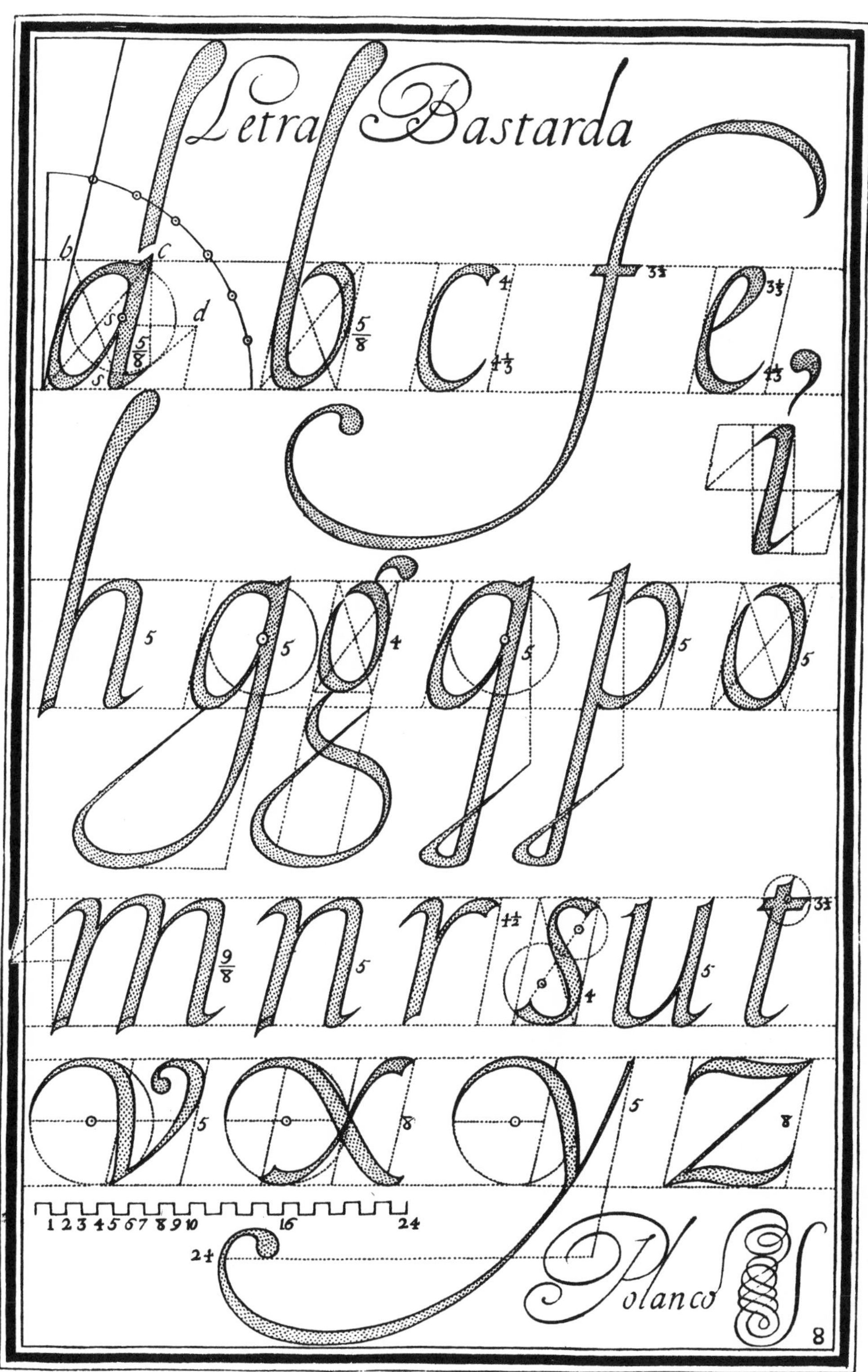

PLATE 133: Polanco, Madrid, 1719

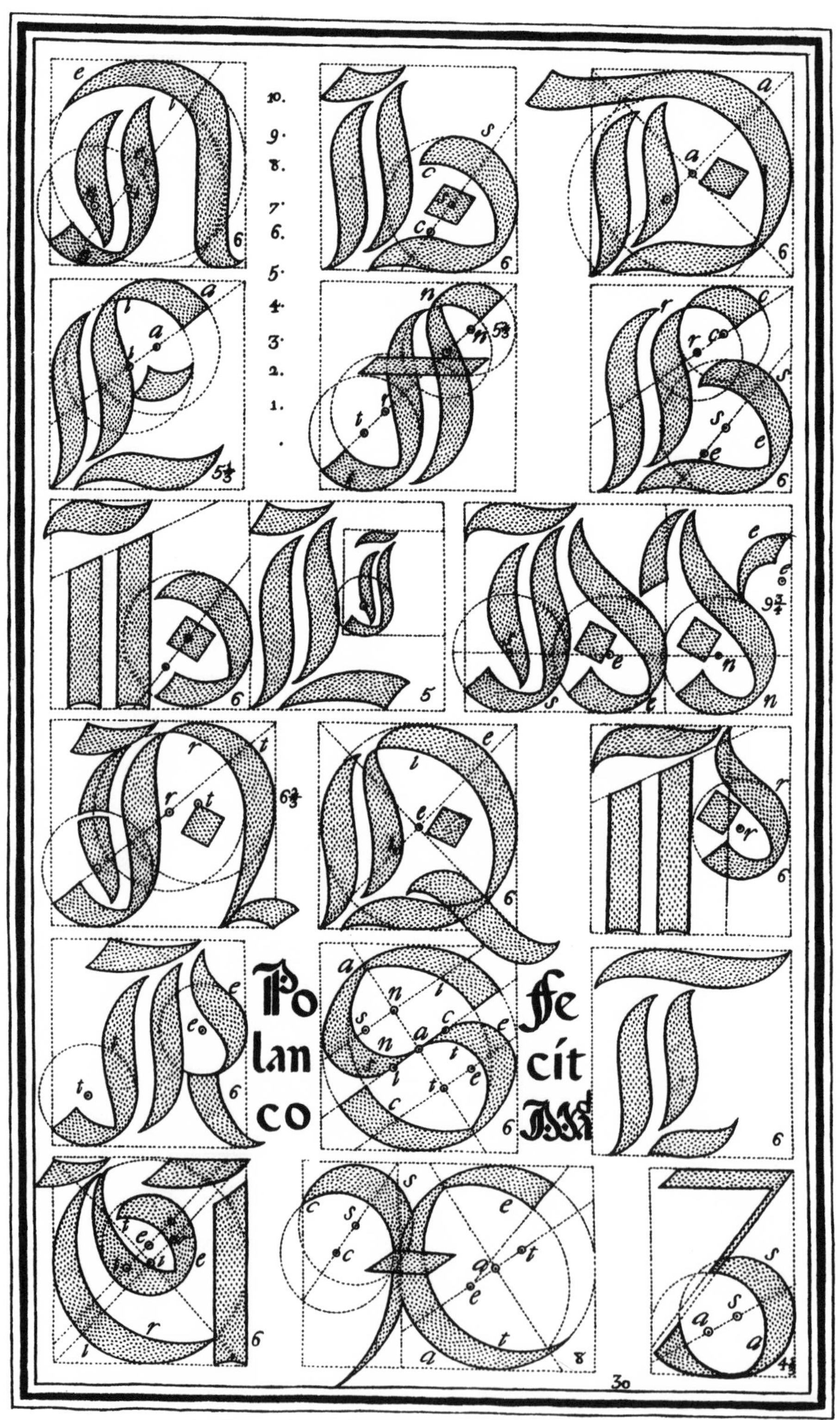

PLATE 134: Polanco, Madrid, 1719

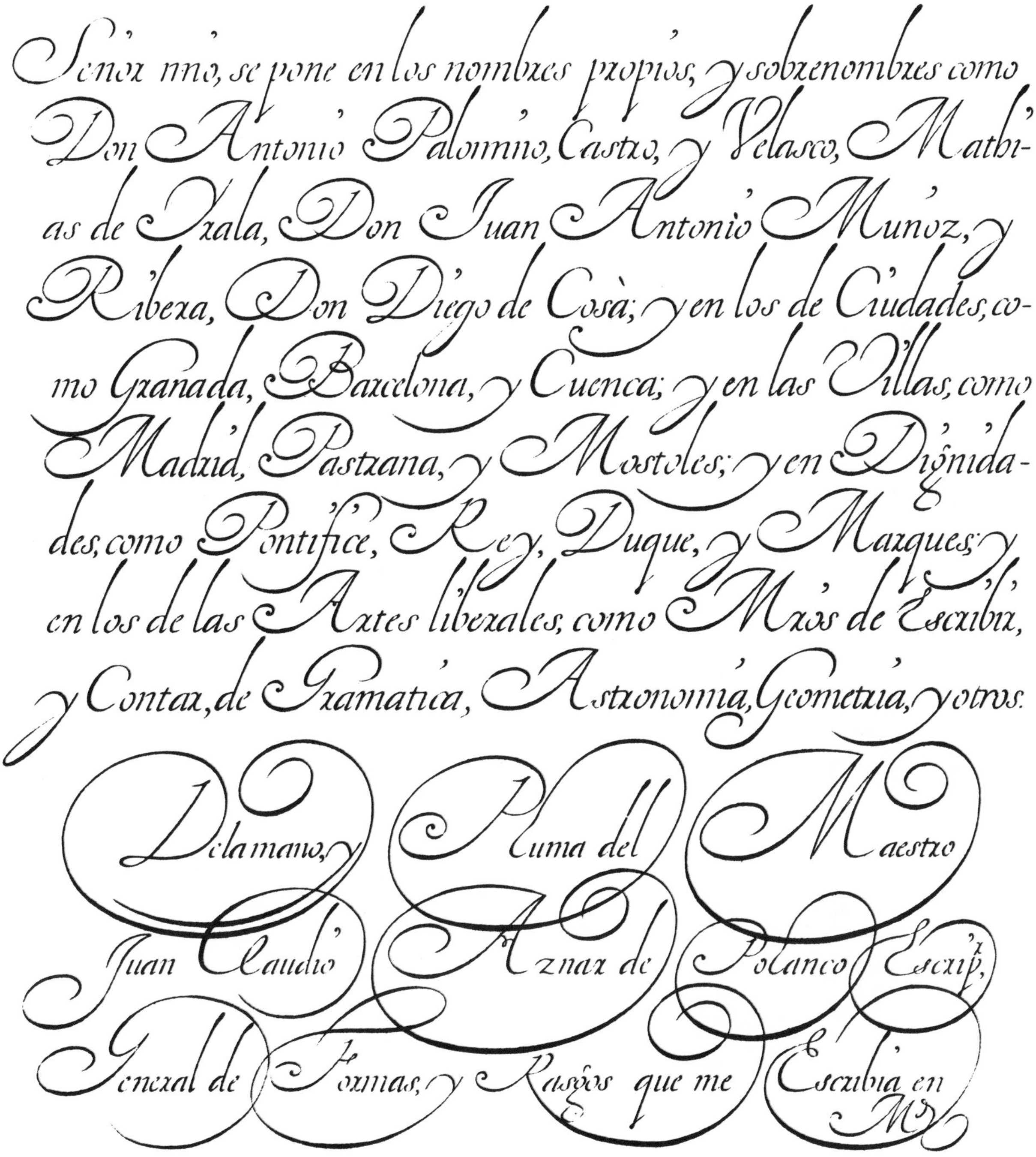

Señor mio, se pone en los nombres propios, y sobrenombres como Don Antonio Palomino, Castro, y Velasco, Mathias de Ayala, Don Juan Antonio Muñoz, y Ribera, Don Diego de Cosà; y en los de Ciudades, como Granada, Barcelona, y Cuenca; y en las Villas, como Madrid, Pastrana, y Mostoles; y en Dignidades, como Pontifice, Rey, Duque, y Marques; y en los de las Artes liberales, como Mros de Escribir, y Contar, de Gramatica, Astronomia, Geometria, y otros.

De la mano, y Pluma del Maestro Juan Claudio Aznar de Polanco Escrip. General de Formas, y Rasgos que me Escribia en Md.

Plate 135: Polanco, Madrid, 1719

Grundstriche der Currentbuchstaben.

Zertheil- und Zerlegung der Current.

Gemeine Fügung der Currentschrift.

Current Versal Alfabet.

N°. 0. 1. 2. 3. 4. 5. 6. 7. 8. 9. 10. 234.

PLATE 136: Spreng, Basel, 1709

Kindliche Liebe, Treü und schuldiger Gehorsam
seye eüch jeder Zeit zuvor, freündl. lieber Vatter!

Gegen Abend den 14.ten Febr. bin ich glücklich, frisch und
gesünd allhier angelangt, und alsobald bey meinem Kost-
herr, und Frauen eingetretten: die seind freündliche, gü-
te Leüte, haben mich bisher also gehalten, dass mich
über selbige zu beklagen keine Ursach habe. Welches
eüch hiemit berichten sollen, den Allmächtigen Gott bit-
tend: dass er eüch sämtlich bey guter Gesündheit erhal-
ten wolle. Geben zu Basel den 27.ten Marty, 1709.

Des Vatters

Gehorsamer Sohn
Josua Kleinmann.

PLATE 137: Spreng, Basel, 1709

Nobilissime Vir, Affinis Charissime.

Nolo te celare, mensem jam esse a quo inter Dominum
Johannem Fridelinum, Mercatorem hujus nostræ civi-
tatis celeberrimum, et Filiam meam Catharinam na-
tu maximam, bonorum amicorum consilio, Sponsalia
sint contracta. Cum igitur tempus tandem requirat, ut
illa coram Ecclesiæ nostræ coetu adhibitis piis precib,
solenniter confirmentur et pro more recepto celebren-
tur, diem illis diximus 9. Julii, ad quem vocavi et vo-
co ex meis, intimos, et conjunctissimos, cum autem te
quoque in numero meorum non postremum habeam,
rogo atque obsecro, ut ad diem dictum, cum Tua Cha-
rissima apud Nos N. compareas, precib, aliorum bonorum, pro felici copulandorum auspicio, tuis ad-
jungas, atque præsentia et authoritate Tua, nostras Nu-
ptias promoveas, erit id nobis tam gratum, ut nihil
gratius Vale Datum Norimbergæ 5. Julii A: 1708.

Tuus Totus

A Monsieur
Monsieur Jan Lambert
Marchand de vin à
Ausbourg

PLATE 138: Zunner, Nuremberg, 1709

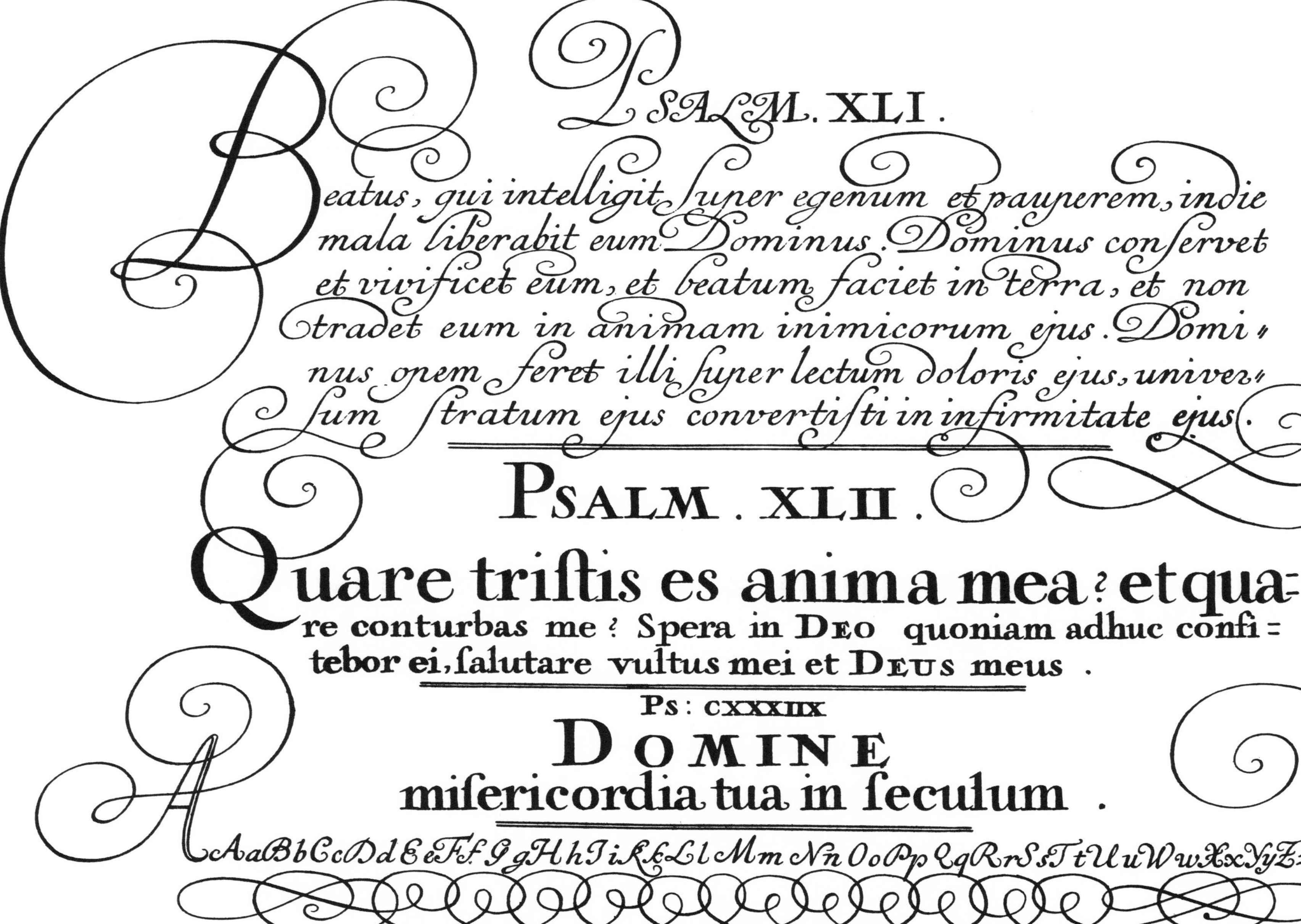

PSALM. XLI.
Beatus, qui intelligit super egenum et pauperem, indie
mala liberabit eum Dominus. Dominus conservet
et vivificet eum, et beatum faciet in terra, et non
tradet eum in animam inimicorum ejus. Domi,
nus opem feret illi super lectum doloris ejus, univer,
sum stratum ejus convertisti in infirmitate ejus.
PSALM . XLII .
Quare tristis es anima mea? et qua=
re conturbas me? Spera in DEO quoniam adhuc confi=
tebor ei, salutare vultus mei et DEUS meus .
Ps: CXXXIIX
DOMINE
misericordia tua in seculum .
AaBbCcDdEeFfGgHhIiKkLlMmNnOoPpQqRrSsTtUuWwXxYyZz.

PLATE 139: Zunner, Nuremberg, 1709

PLATE 140: C. Brunner, Basel, 1730

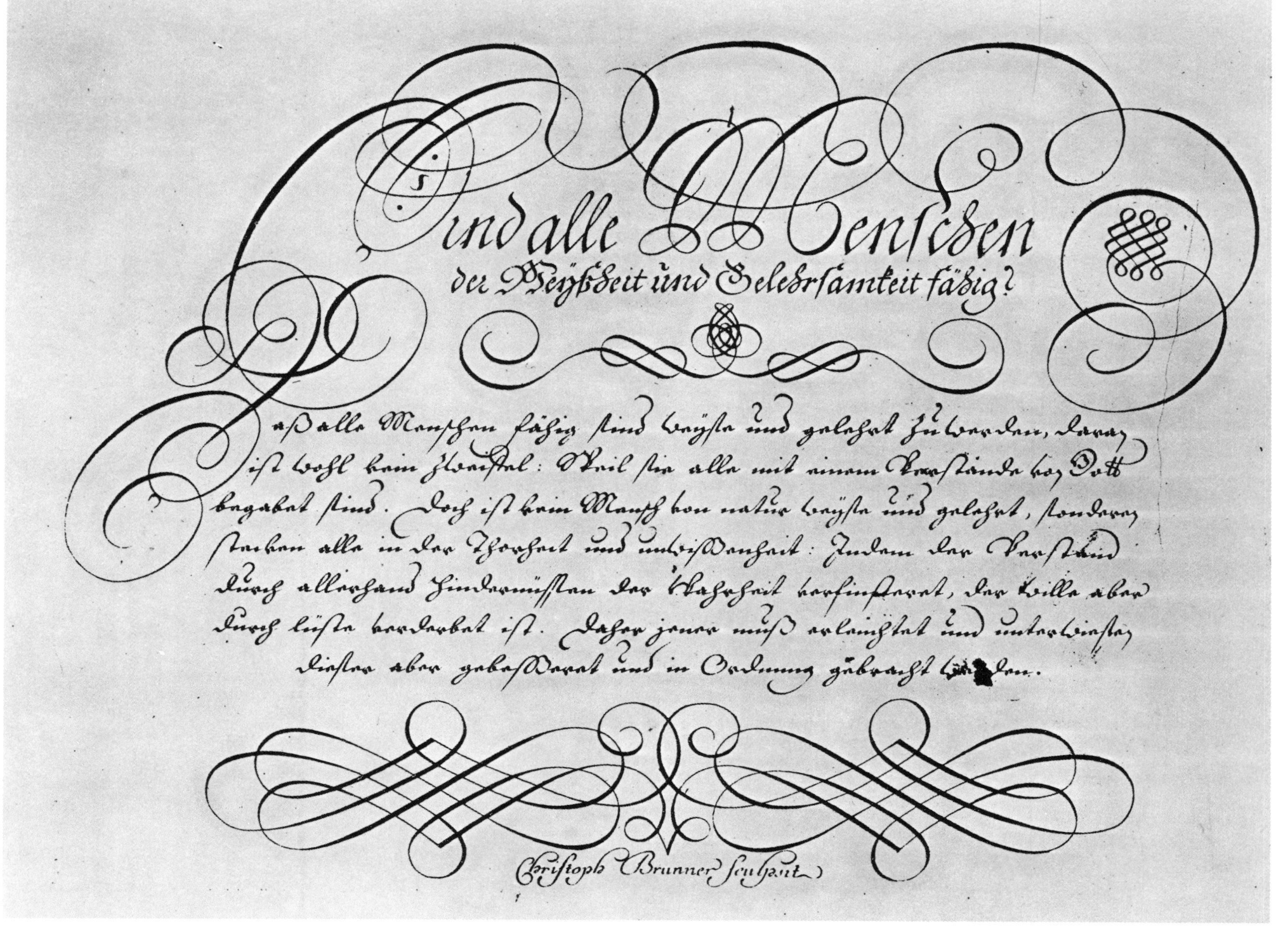

PLATE 141: C. Brunner, Basel, 1729

A Basle le 30 7bre 1729.

Monsieur

Remarqués s'il Vous plait qu'il faut pour cette Ecriture Courante ou d'Expe
dition tenir la Plume haute beaucoup sur l'obliq, observant de ne point remonter
Vos liaisons sur les jambages des Lettres m et n quant au surplus des autres
Caractaires il faut au contraire descendre les jambages sur les liaisons, s'appliq
d'ailleurs a donner autant qu'il sera possible des distances egalles tant d'un
mot à un autre & d'une ligne à une autre sans faire aucune poche aux lettres
qui ont testes et queües. C'est l'avis de Celuy qui est

Monsieur

Vre Serviteur
Brunner

PLATE 142: C. Brunner, Basel, 1729

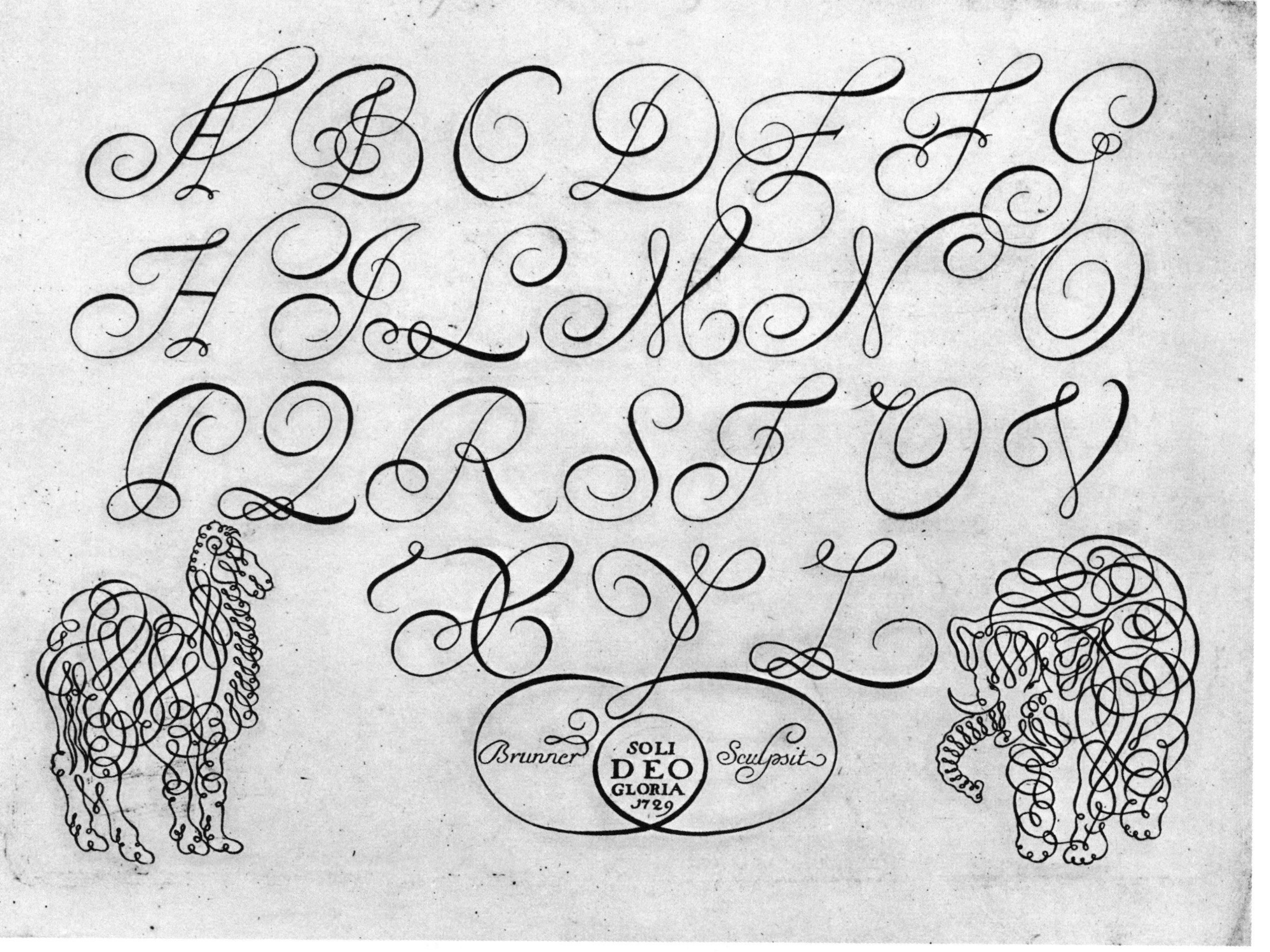

Plate 143: C. Brunner, Basel, 1729

So verblyd u, jongeling, in uwe jeugd, en laat uw herte vrolyk zyn in uwe jeugd: doet wat uw herte lust, en uwen ogen behaagt; en weet-dat u God om dit alles sal voor't gerigte doen Komen.
Laat de treurigheyd uyt uw herte, en doet het quade weg van uw Lighaam: want de Kindsheyd en jeugd is ydelheyd. Gedenkt aan uwen Schepper in uwe jeugd. Prediker Salomons. Cap. 12. v. 1. 2. 3.

Gott, der dich und mich gemacht,
Gott, den geber aller Gaben,
Must du stets vor Augen haben;
Er g..bt auch auf dich stets acht.
Freue dich in deiner Jugend;
Aber denck auch an die Tugend;
Weil du Gott bey deiner Lust
Red und Antwort geben must

PLATE 144: Bland, n.p., 1739

Pseaume CXXVII.
CXXVIII Selon les Hebreux.

1 Heureux sont tous ceux qui craignent le Seigneur, et
qui marchent dans ses voïes.
2 Vous mangerez le fruit des travaux de vos mains et en
cela vous êtes heureux; et vous le serés encore a l'avenir.
3 Vôtre femme sera dans le secret de vôtre maison comme
une vigne abondante qui porte beaucoup de fruit.
Vos enfans seront tout au tour de vôtre table comme
de jeunes Oliviers.
4 C'est ainsi que sera beni l'homme qui craint le Seigneur.
5 Que le Seigneur vous benisse de Sion, afin que vous
contempliés les biens de Jerusalem pendant tous les
jours de vôtre vie.
6 Et que vous voyez les enfans de vos enfans, et la paix
en Israël.

PLATE 145: Bland, n.p., 1739

Omnium rerum Vanitas.

Omne hoc Spatium, cui tanta nomina
imponitis, quod Europam, Asiam, Africam
Americam dixistis, in quo misere erratis,
ut vivatis miserius, in quo navigatis, itis,
festinatis, curritis, in cujus parte sed exigua
et prope nulla annos decem circulator ille
Homericus jactatus est, si cum toto
conferatur; vix unius horæ iter est. Hoc qui
capit, nunquam æstimabit vitam; nunquam
formidabit mortem; Nunquam enim totum se
in angustias has dabit, qui tam magna sui
parte, animo nempe, terram jam excessit.

PLATE 146: Bland, n.p., 1739.

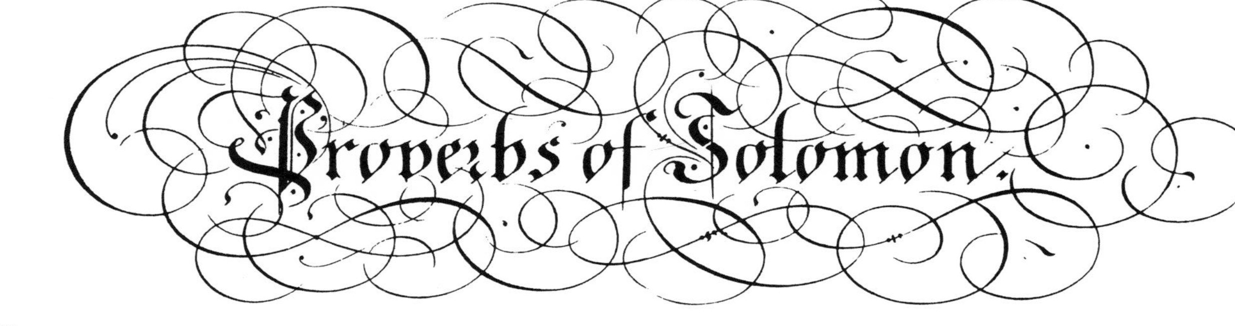

Happy is the man that findeth Wisdom, and the man that
getteth Understanding. For the Merchandise of it is better than the
Merchandise of Silver, and the gain thereof than fine Gold. She
is more precious than Rubies: and all the things thou canst desire
are not to be compared unto her: Length of days is in her right hand
and in her left hand Riches and Honour. Her ways are ways of
pleasantness and all her paths are Peace. Chap. 3. Ver. 13 &c.

Bland Scr.

PLATE 147: Bland, n.p., 1739

Rom. 8. v. 11.

But if the Spirit of him that raised up Jesus from the dead,
dwell in you; he that raised up Christ from the dead, shall also
quicken your mortal bodies, by his Spirit that dwelleth in you.

Daniel 12. v. 2. 3.

And many of them that sleep in the dust of the Earth shall awake,
some to everlasting Life; and some to shame and everlasting Contempt:
And they that be wise shall shine as the brightneſs of the firmament;
and they that turn many to Righteousneſs, as the Stars for ever and ever:

Geist des Lebens wohn in mir!
Stelle mir nebst meinem Grabe
Den erstandenen Heiland für,
Daſs ich Lust zu ſterben habe!

Wer durch dich versichert ist,
Daſs er wieder auferwacht:
Der erschrickt nicht vor der Nacht
Die uns Aug und Leben schliest!

PLATE 148: Bland. n.p., 1739

Monsieur Londres le 18.me May 1739.

Puisque vous avés tant attandû je vous prie d'avoir encore patience jus-
qu'à la Semaine prochaine; je vous proteste que je suis dans le dernier Chagrin de
vous avoir si souvent manqué de Parole: Vous êtes le premier, qui s'est plaint de
Moi, car je veux bien que vous sçachiés que je suis honeste Homme & que je ne trompe
Personne. Il est vrai que la somme n'est pas grande c'est pourquoi vous devés croire
que c'est à mon Regret si je ne vous ai pas payé si tot que je l'aurois souhaité, j'en
aurois de la Confusion si c'étoit ma Faute. Je vous prie de ne me pas traiter avec
la derniere Severité, si vous voulés que je continue à etre.

A Monsieur
M.r Cons. Jaques Lommineaux
March.d à
Bourdeaux.

Monsieur
Votre tres humble & tres obeissant Serviteur
Jean Bavoix

PLATE 149: Bland, n.p., 1739

Round Text Copies;

By Willington Clark,

of Christ-Church Southwark.

Aaabbbccddeeffffgghhhijkkklllmm

nnoopppqrrrsſsttttuvvnnvxxyyzzz.

ABCDEFGHIKLM

NOPQRSTUVWXYZ.

Authority. Barbarity. Centurions.

Demands. Encomium. Fraternity.

PLATE 150: Bickham, London, 1743

Aim at improvement in every line.

Busineſs makes a Man respected.

Commendation animates the mind.

Diligence in youth is commendable.

Exceſs produceth great prodigality.

Friendship improves Happineſs.

PLATE 151: Bickham, London, 1743

Let your Promises be sincere; and so Prudently considered as not to exceed the reach of your Ability; He who Promises more than he is Able to Perform is False to himself; and he who does not Perform what he has Promised, is a Traytor to his Friend.

Your Promises once made are past Debate;
And Truth's of more Necessity than Fate.
N. Dove Scrip.

PLATE 152: Bickham, London, 1743

To the Right Honourable the
Lord-Mayor, and Court of Aldermen,
Of the City of London.
A B C D E F G H I
To the Hon.ble the Sub-Governor,
Deputy-Governor, and Directors of
the South-Sea Company.
J K L M N O P Q R
To the Honourable the
Governor, Deputy-Governor, and Directors
Of the Bank of England.
S T V U W X Y Z Z.
Invented, & Written by Joseph Champion
Master of the Boarding-School, in
King's-Head-Court, St. Paul's Church-Yard.

PLATE 153: Bickham, London, 1743

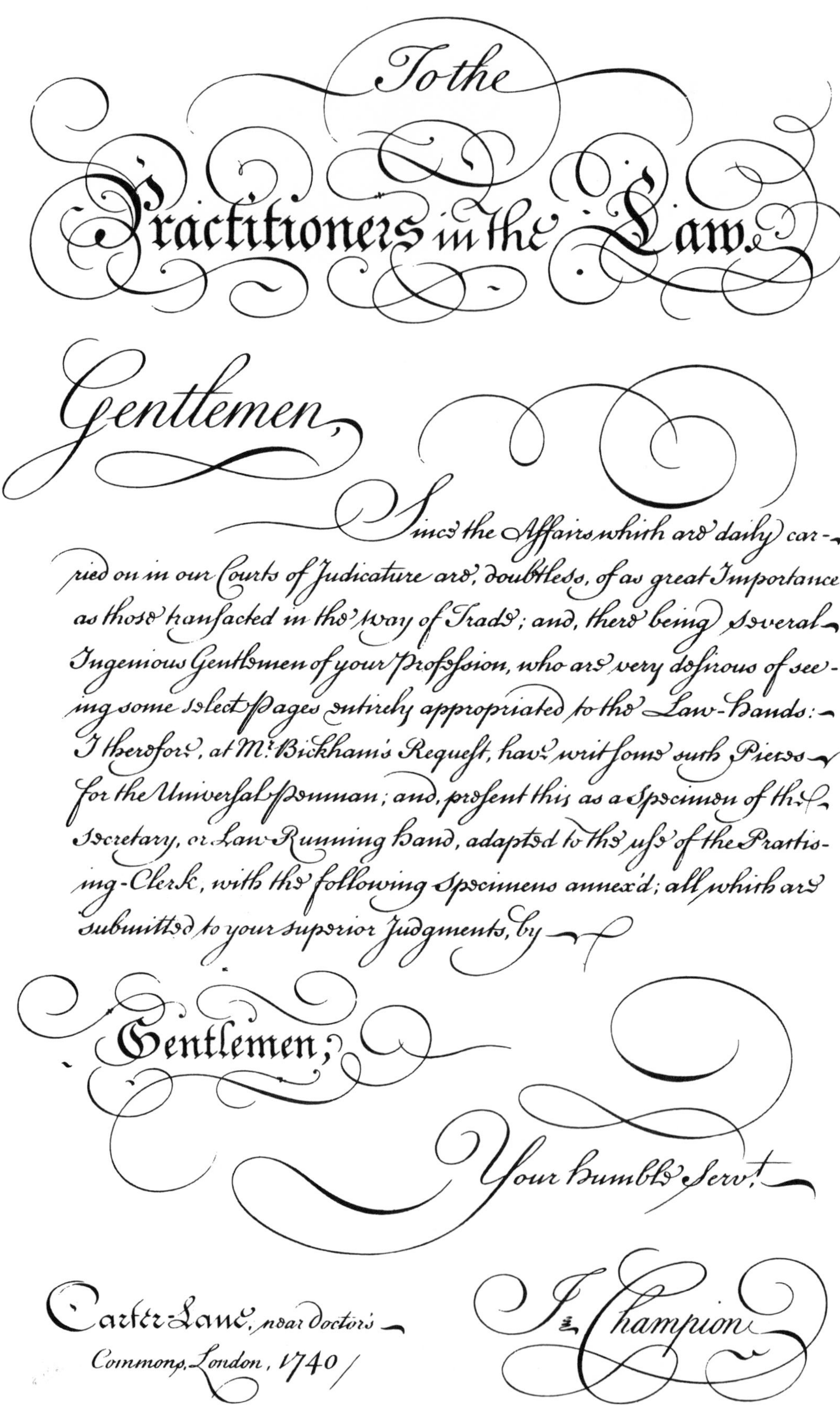

To the Practitioners in the Law.

Gentlemen,

Since the Affairs which are daily carried on in our Courts of Judicature are, doubtless, of as great Importance as those transacted in the Way of Trade; and, there being several Ingenious Gentlemen of your Profession, who are very desirous of seeing some select Pages entirely appropriated to the Law-Hands: I therefore, at Mr. Bickham's Request, have writ some such Pieces for the Universal Penman; and, present this as a Specimen of the Secretary, or Law-Running hand, adapted to the use of the Practising-Clerk, with the following Specimens annex'd; all which are submitted to your superior Judgments, by

Gentlemen,

Your humble Servt.

J. Champion

Carter-Lane, near Doctor's Commons, London, 1740.

PLATE 154: Bickham, London, 1743

Of all the Cauſes which conſpire to blind
Man's erring Judgment & misguide the Mind,
What yͤ weak Head with ſtrongeſt Biaſs rules
Is Pride, the never-failing Vice of Fools.

Pride hides a Man's faults from himſelf, and magnifies them to others.

Whatever Nature has in Worth deny'd,
She gives in large recruits of needful Pride;
Pride, where Wit fails, ſteps in to our defence,
And fills up all the mighty Void of Senſe.

PLATE 155: Bickham, London, 1743

The Alphabets *in all Hands, Engrav'd by* George Bickham.

German Text.

Round Text.

Square Text.

Round Hand.

Engrossing.

Secretary.

Joseph Champion scr.

Sold by Henry Overton at the White Horse without Newgate London

PLATE 156: Bickham, London, 1743

Old English Print.

Aabcdefghijklmnopqrſsſtuvwxyz.&c.

A B C D E F G H I J K L M N O P

Q R S T U W X Y Z Z. J. C.

Italick Print.

Aabcdefghijklmnopqrſstuvwwxyz.æœ.

A B C D E F G H I J K L M N O P Q R

R S T U V W X Y Y Z Æ.

Roman Print.

Aabcdefghijklmnopqrſstuvwxyz.

ABCDEFGHIJKLMNOPQ

Italian Hand.

aabbccddeeffffgghhijkkllmmnoppqrsſsttuvwxyzz.

A B C D E F G H I J K L L M M N

N O P Q R S T U V W W X X Y Z Z.

Court Hand.

[Court Hand alphabet]

The Chancery.

Aa Bb Cc Dd Ee Ffff Gg Hh Iij Kk Ll Mm Nn

Oo Pp Qq Rr Sſs Tt Uuv Ww Xx Yy Zz.&c. Champion Scrip.

PLATE 157: Bickham, London, 1743

General Lopez wollte sich vor einer Action seinen Helm
von seinem Bedienten besser aufsetzen lassen, er drücke
ihm das Ohr: Man behauptete, es könne nicht seyn, der
Helm sitze recht, und Lopez, um nichts zu versäumen, eilte
ins Treffen. Bey seiner Zurückkunft warf er den Helm und
das Ohr zugleich ins Zimmer, und sagte ganz gelassen zu seinen Bedienten: habe ich nicht gesagt, dass mein Helm nicht recht sitze:

a a b b c c d d e e f ff g g h h ch ch i i k ck l ll m m n n o o p p p q q r r
s ss st ß r t tt u ü v v w w x x y ÿ z tz z

Menzzer scripsit

Coentgen sculps.

PLATE 158: Menzzer, Darmstadt, 1775

Canzley Alphabet.

am, bm, cm, dm, em, fm, gm, hm, im, km, lm, mm, nm, om, pm, qm, rm, ſm, tm,
ům, vm, wm, ym, ÿm, zm.

Menzzer scripsit.

Coentgen sculpsit.

PLATE 159: Menzzer, Darmstadt, 1775

Principes de l'Ecriture
Françoise.
Ecriture Posée.
a b c d d e f g g h h j i l m n o p q r ſ s t u v v æ x y z z.
Ecriture Coulée, Courante ou d'Expédition.
Ecriture Coulée, Courante ou d'Expédition.
A B C D E F G H I L M N O P Q R S T U V X Y Z B
Gravons dans le Marbre et l'Airain, Que Dieu seul est le Souverain,
Et que toute la Terre est pleine De sa Majesté souveraine

PLATE 160: Braun, Mulhouse, 1774

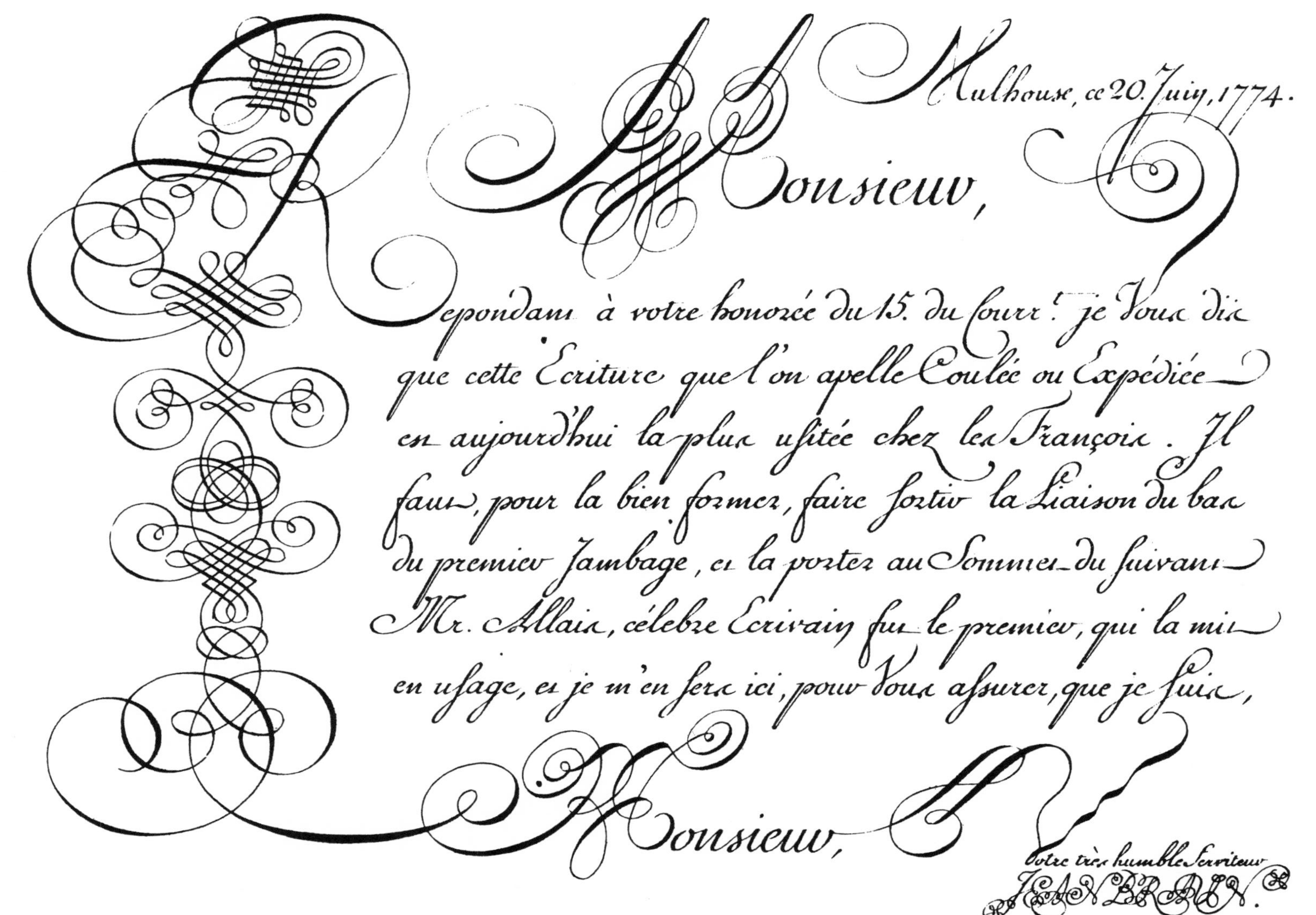

Mulhouse, ce 20. Juin, 1774.

Monsieur,

Repondant à votre honorée du 15. du courr.t je Vous dis que cette Écriture que l'on apelle Coulée ou Expédiée est aujourd'hui la plus usitée chez les François. Il faut, pour la bien former, faire sortir la Liaison du bas du premier Jambage, et la porter au Sommet du suivant. Mr. Allais, célebre Ecrivain fut le premier, qui la mit en usage, et je m'en sers ici, pour Vous assurer, que je suis,

Monsieur,

Votre très humble Serviteur
JEAN BRAUN.

PLATE 161: Braun, Mulhouse, 1774

PLATE 162: Braun, Mulhouse, 1774

schen, so er die ganze Welt gewonne, u.
nähme doch Schaden an seiner Seele? oder

PLATE 163: Braun, Mulhouse, 1774

PLATE 164: J. J. Brunner, Berne, 1766

En Main levée.
Gravé par C. G. Gouttenberg 1767.

PLATE 165: J. J. Brunner, Berne, 1766

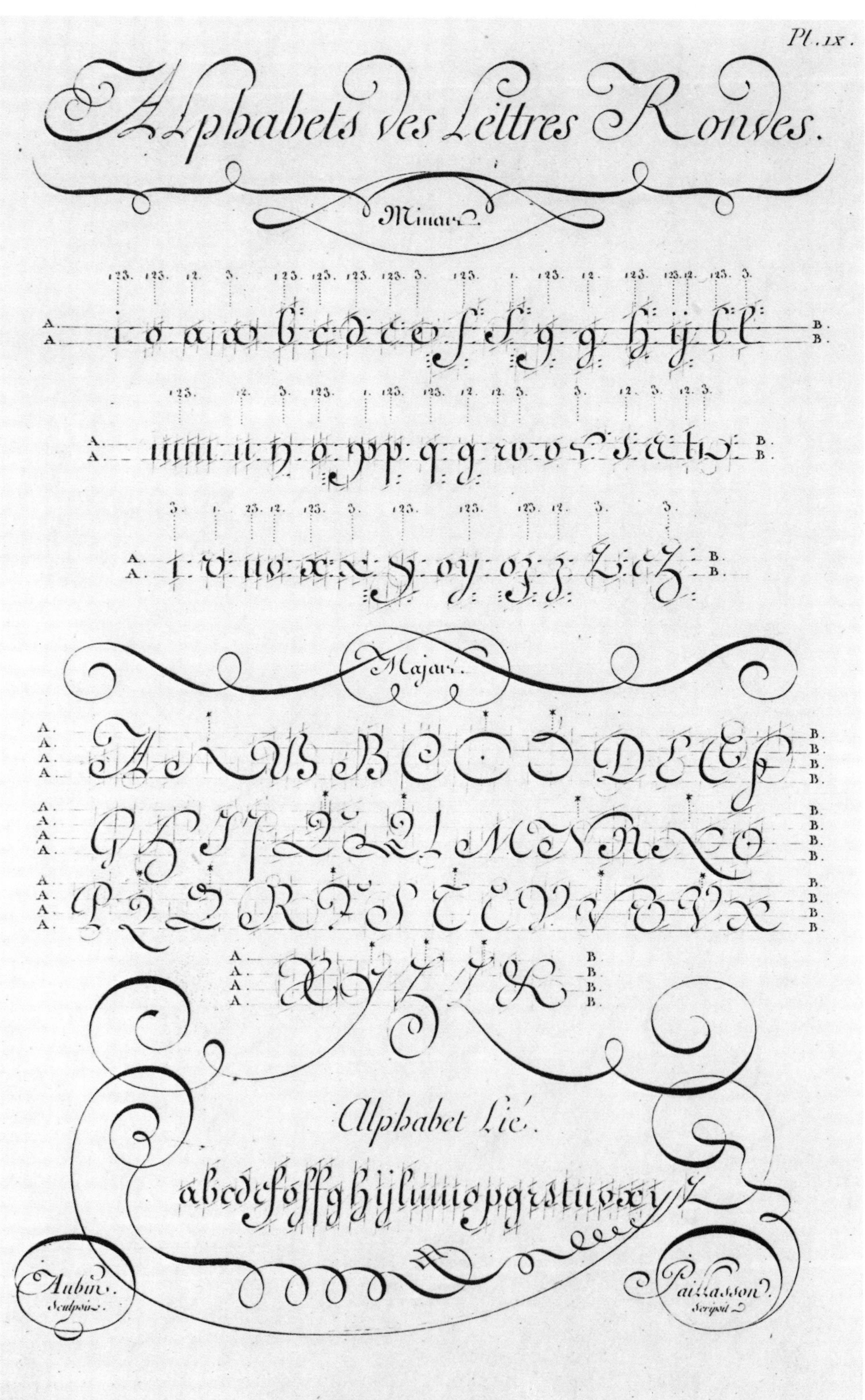

PLATE 166: Paillasson, Paris, 1760

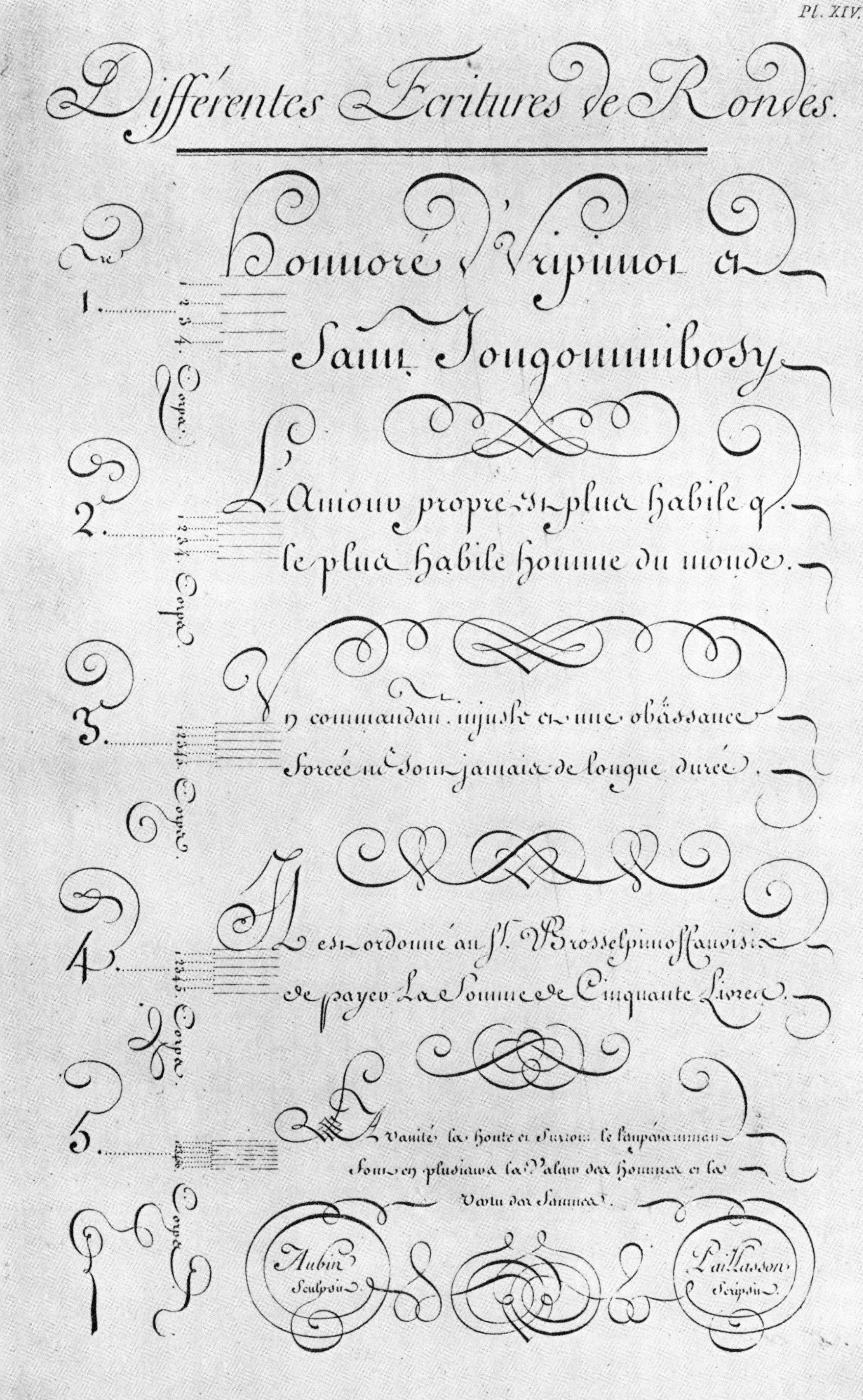

PLATE 167: Paillasson, Paris, 1760

PLATE 168: Paillasson, Paris, 1760

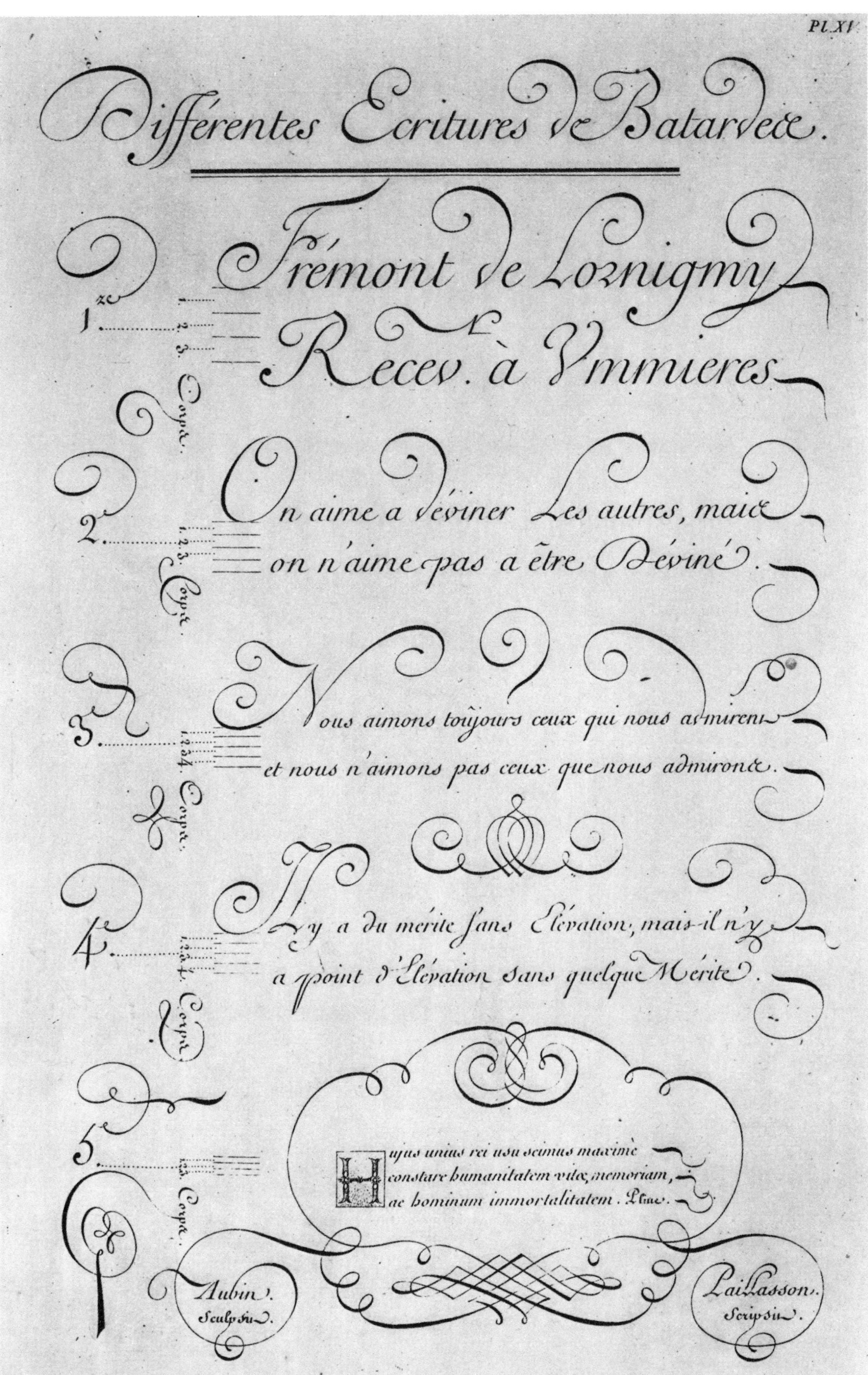

PLATE 169: Paillasson, Paris, 1760

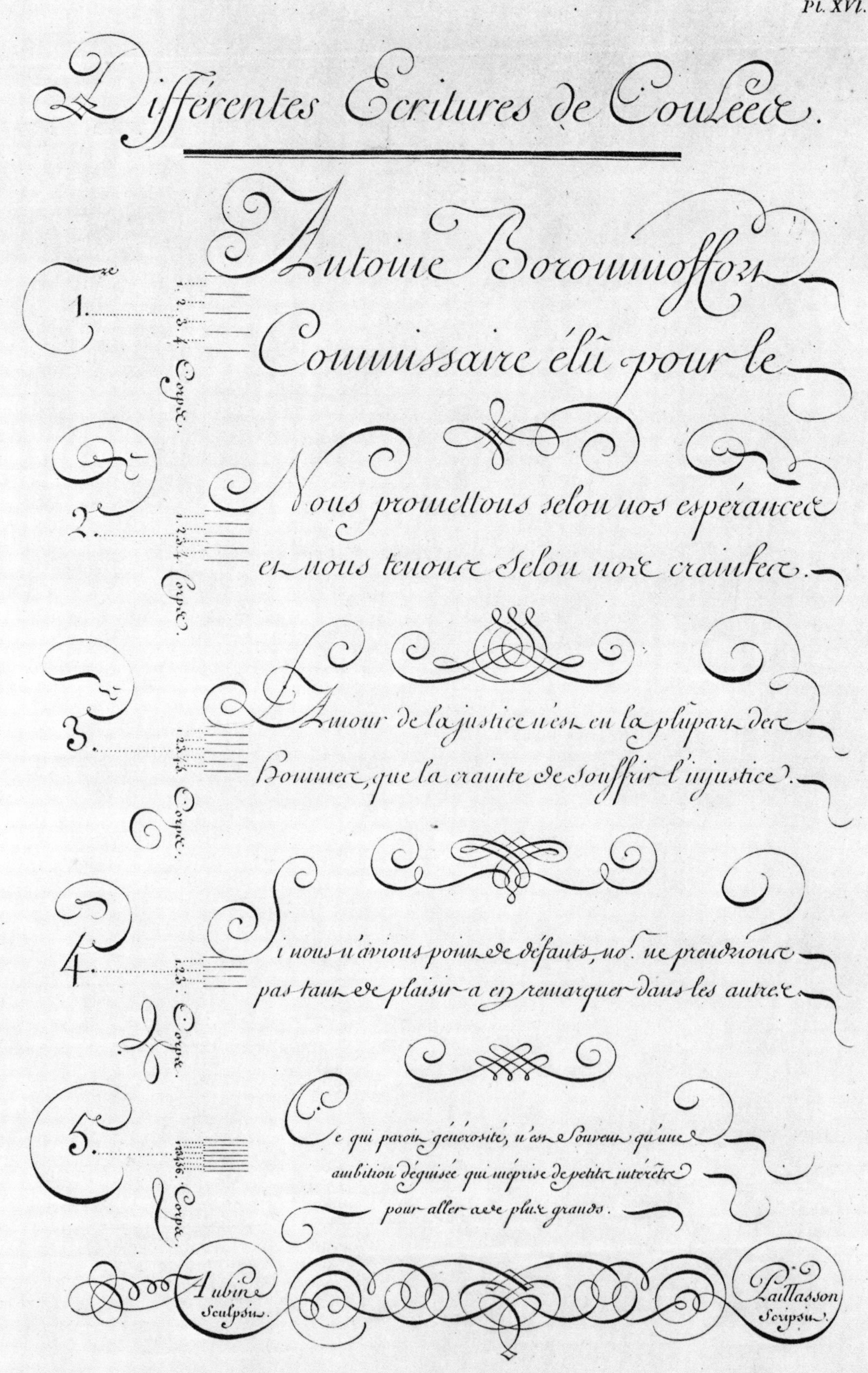

PLATE 170: Paillasson, Paris, 1760

PLATE 171: Paillasson, Paris, 1760

PLATE 172: Paillasson, Paris, 1760

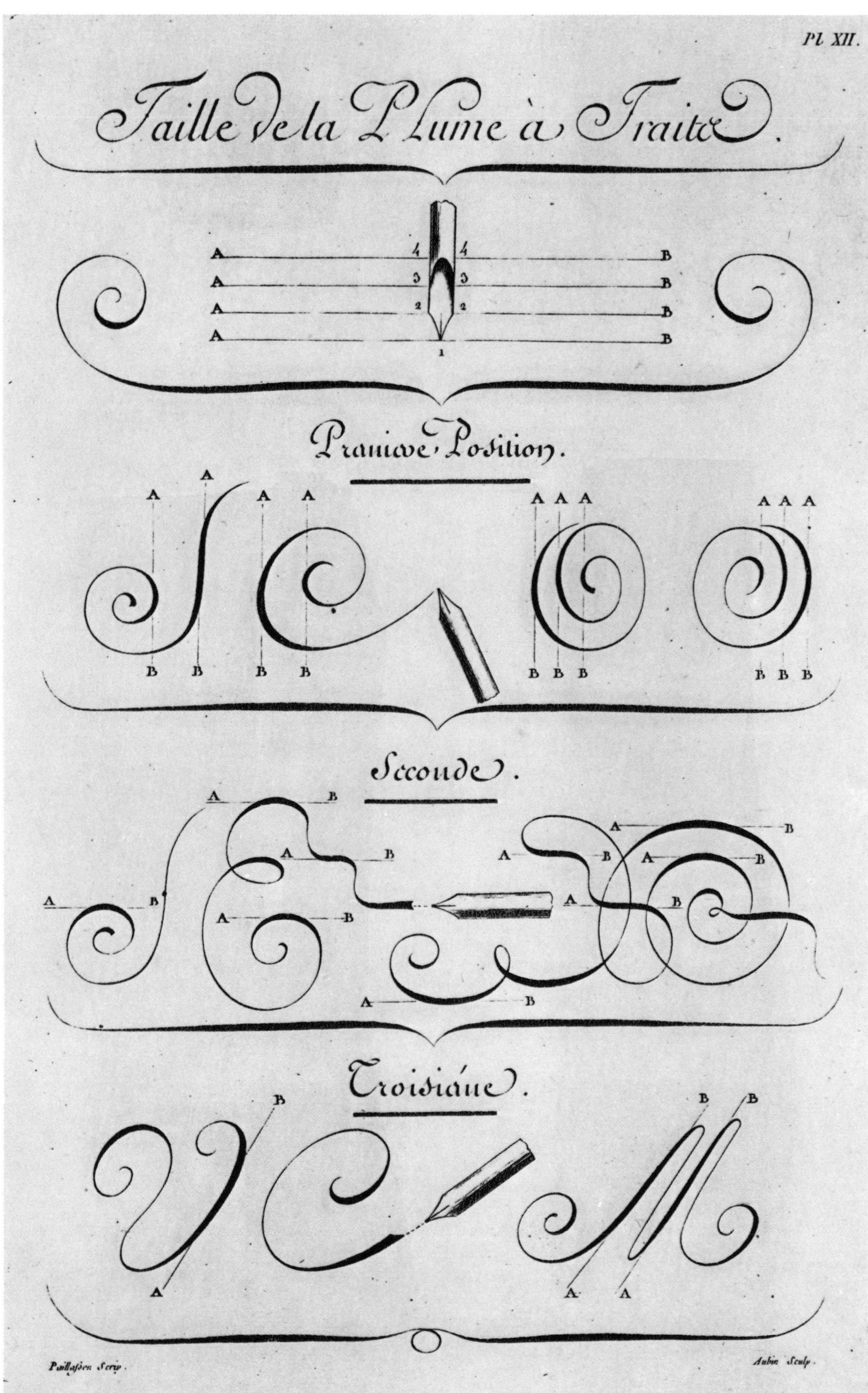

PLATE 173: Paillasson, Paris, 1760

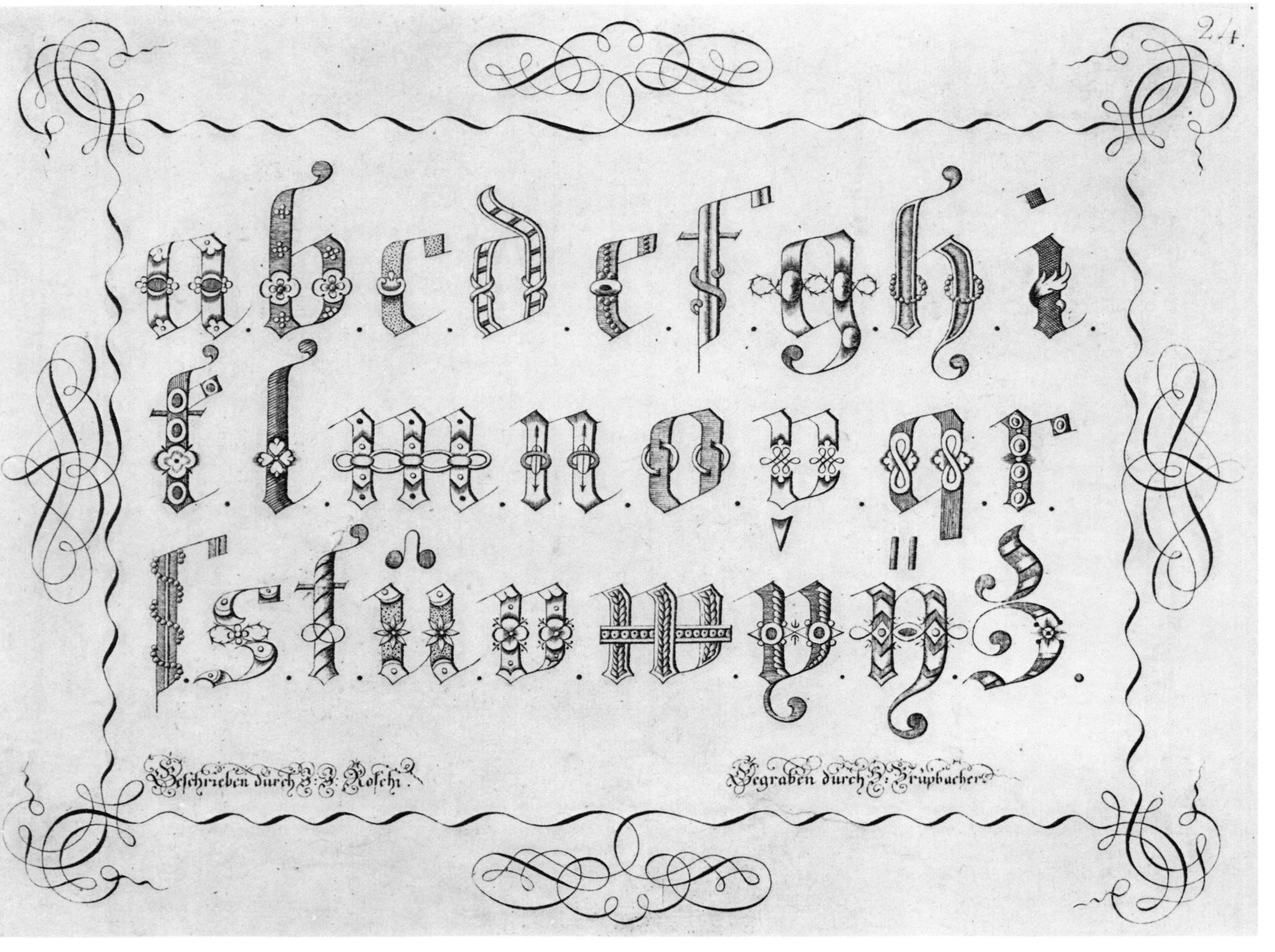

PLATE 174: Roschi, Berne, 1789

PLATE 175: Roschi, Berne, 1789

Grund der Current-Schrift.

1. 2. 3. 3. 4. 5. 6. 7. 8. 9. 0.

PLATE 176: *Vorschriften*, Winterthur, 1805.

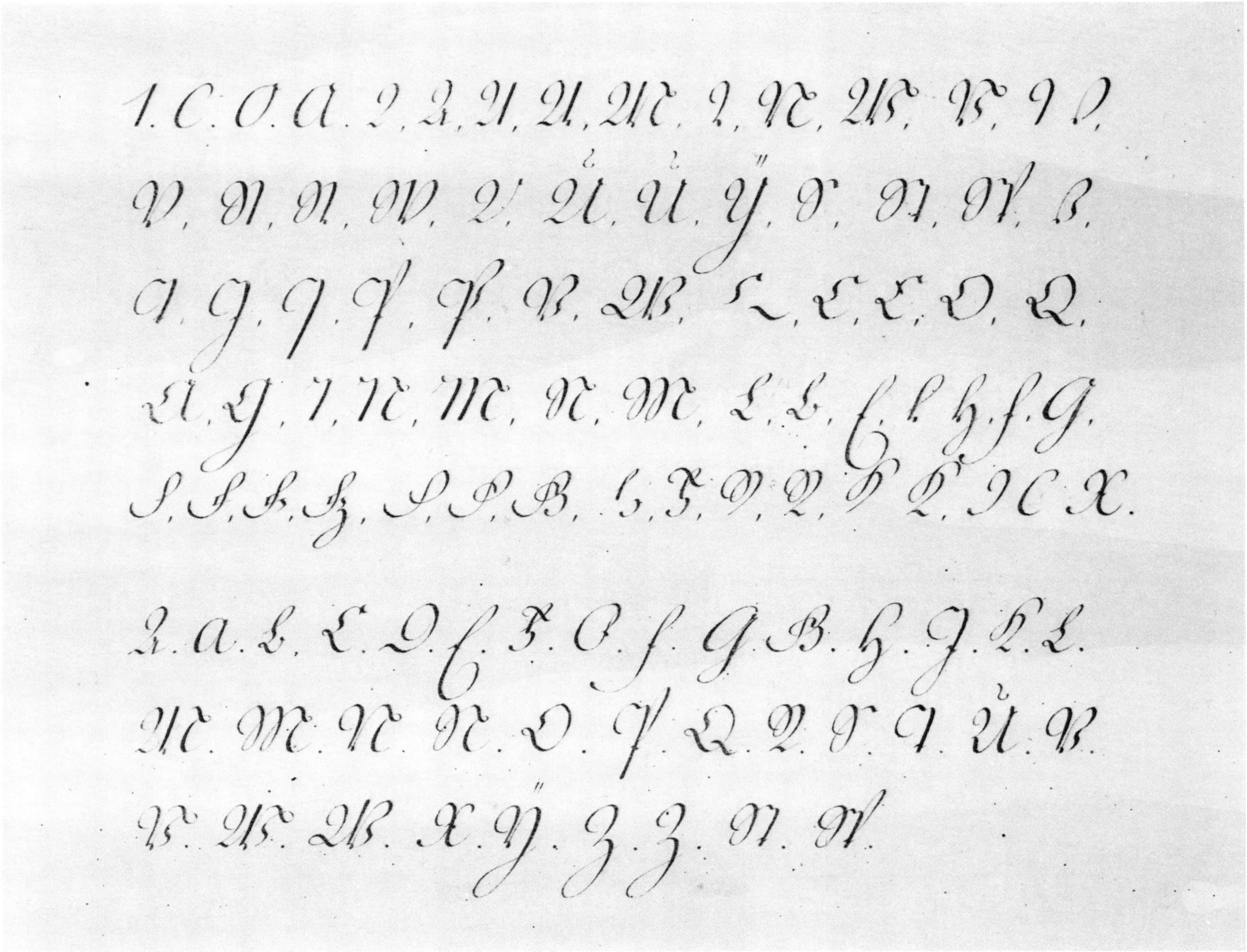

PLATE 177: *Vorschriften*, Winterthur, 1805

Gründ der Canzley-Schrift

Versal-Buchstaben, u: Gründstriche

PLATE 178: *Vorschriften*, Winterthur, 1805

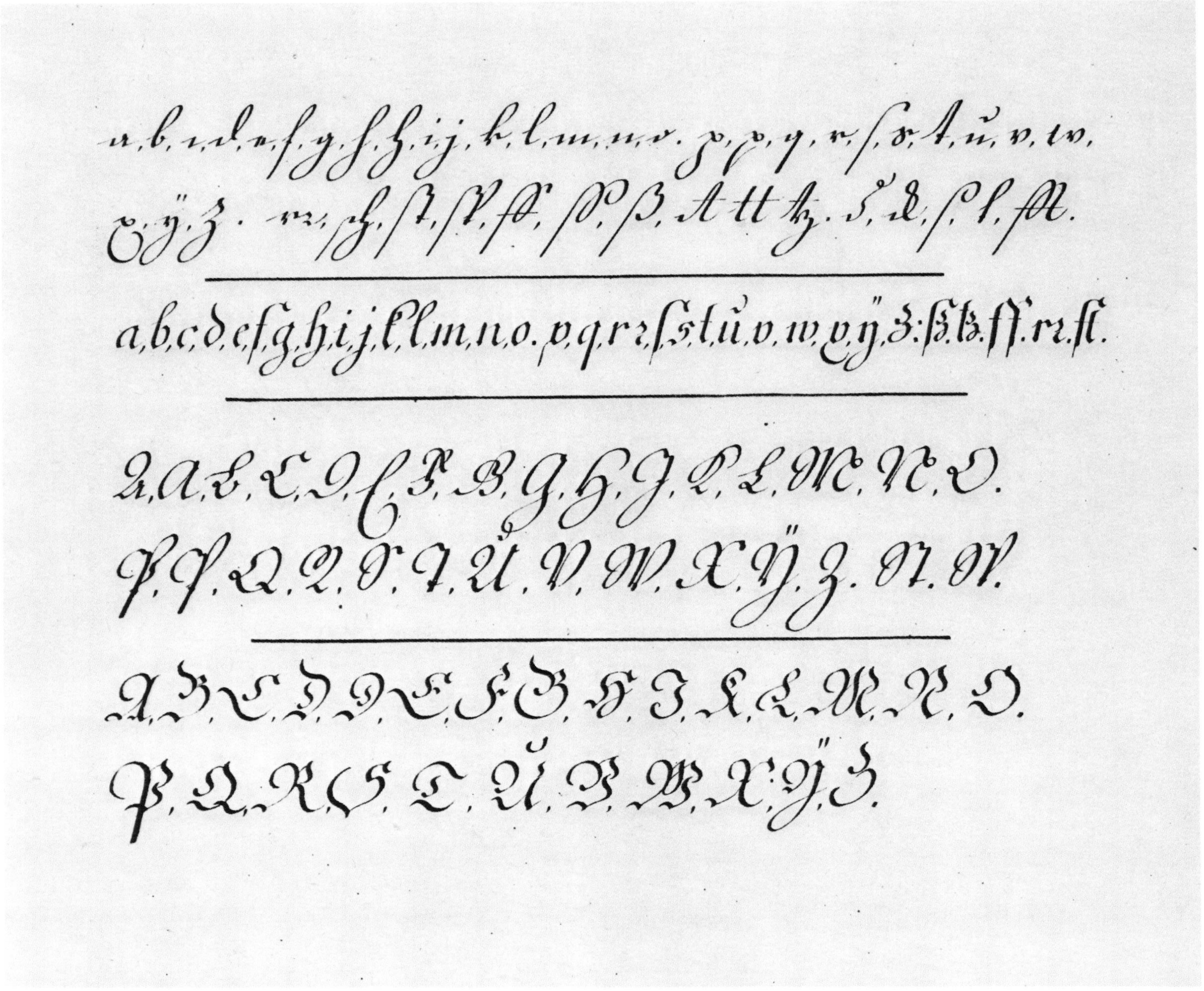

PLATE 179: *Vorschriften*, Winterthur, 1805

N. 11.

Nütze deine Jugendjahre, und lerne fleißig und gern.
O, wie mancher würde gern lernen, wenn er die
Zeit und den Unterricht hätte, den du hast!

Im Alter bereüt man zu spät, daß man in der Jugend die Anläße und Gelegenheiten, sich Kenntniße
und Wißenschaften zu erwerben, vernachläßigt hat.

Fliehe böse Gesellschaften; denn böse Reden und böse
Beyspiele verderben gute Sitten. Suche hingegen mit
allem Ernst den Umgang tugendhafter Personen.

PLATE 180: *Vorschriften*, Winterthur, 1805

La sincerité, quoique très rare dans ce monde est
pourtant une vertu très necessaire, car l'imposture et
le mensonge ne conviennent qu'à des ames basses.
Les gens du monde mettent pour le premier principe
de leur morale, qu'il faut cacher sous de faux dehors
ce qu'on a de plus secret dans le coeur: qu'un hom=
me qui ne sait pas se déguiser ne doit pas espérer
de faire fortune. 1. 2. 3. 4. 5. 6. 7. 8. 9. 10.

PLATE 181: *Vorschriften*, Winterthur, 1805

III. Die großen Schreibbuchstaben.

(. C . T . E . D . O . A . Ä . Q . G .

) . Z . S . N . M . R . X . 2 . U . Ü . V . W . Y . J . P .

(. L . B . F . H . K .

Ansbach . Bamberg . Culmbach . Chiemsee . Dillingen . Erlangen . Fürth .

Günzenhausen . Hof . Ingolstadt . Kempten . Lindau . München . Nördlingen .

Ottobeuren . Passau . Philadelphia . Quedlinburg . Regensburg . Schwabach .

Salzburg . Kalt . Straubing . Tyrol . Uffenheim . Vorchheim . Wittelsbach

Xanten . York . Zürmarshausen .

1 . 2 . 3 . 4 . 5 . 6 . 7 . 8 . 9 . 0 . , ; . : ! ? „ —

g. Vogel sc.

PLATE 182: Stephani, Erlangen, 1815

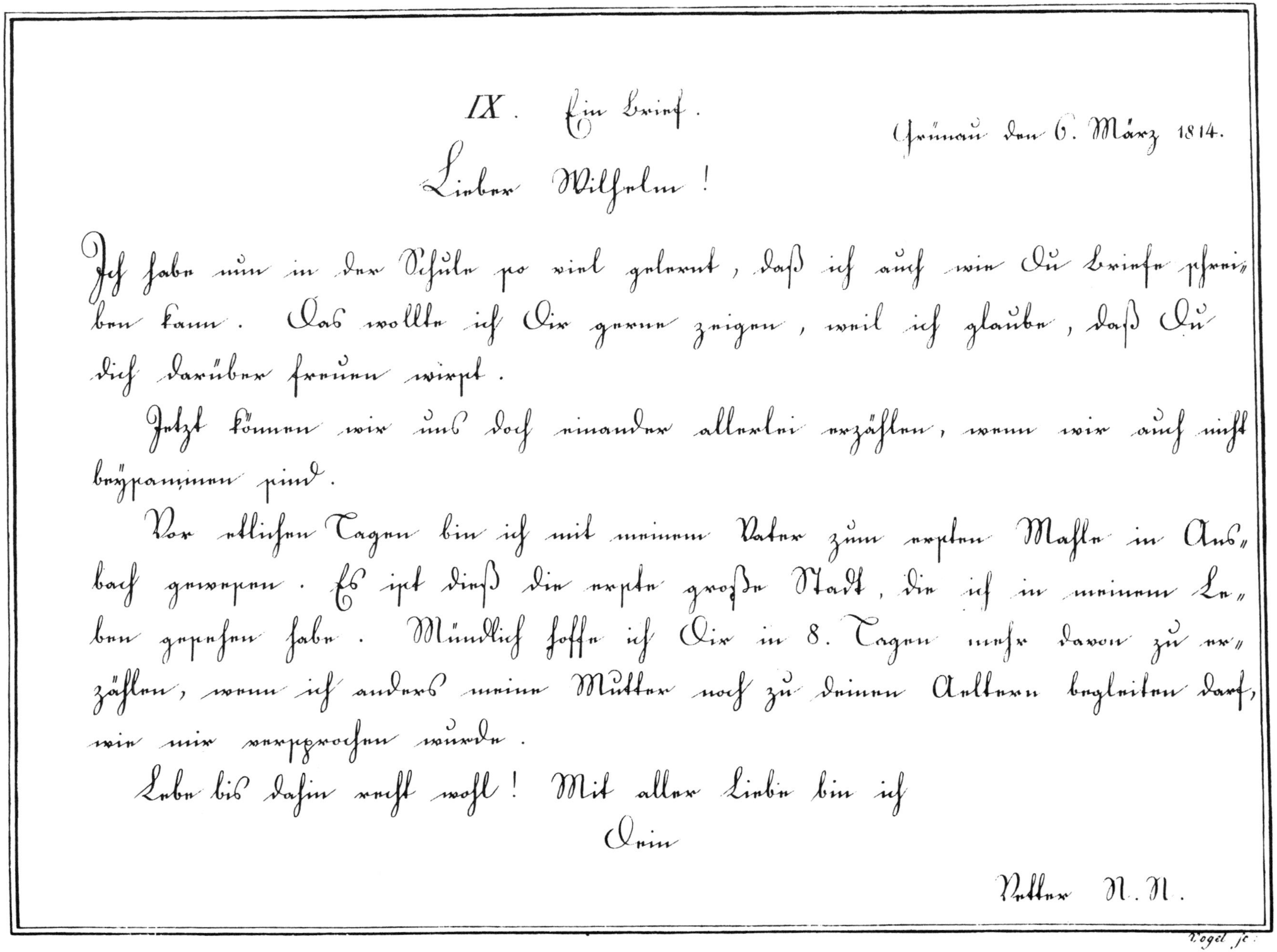

IX. Ein Brief.

Grünau den 6. März 1814.

Lieber Wilhelm!

Ich habe nun in der Schule so viel gelernt, daß ich auch wie Du Briefe schreiben kann. Das wollte ich Dir gerne zeigen, weil ich glaube, daß Du dich darüber freuen wirst.

Jetzt können wir uns doch einander allerlei erzählen, wenn wir auch nicht beysammen sind.

Vor etlichen Tagen bin ich mit meinem Vater zum ersten Male in Ansbach gewesen. Es ist dieß die erste große Stadt, die ich in meinem Leben gesehen habe. Mündlich hoffe ich Dir in 8. Tagen mehr davon zu erzählen, wenn ich anders meine Mutter noch zu deinen Aeltern begleiten darf, wie mir versprochen wurde.

Lebe bis dahin recht wohl! Mit aller Liebe bin ich

Dein

Vetter N. N.

Vogel sc.

PLATE 183: Stephani, Erlangen, 1815

Anweisung.

Herr Blasius Eschmann in Cöln beliebe gegen diese Anweisung an die Verordnung des Herrn Carl Imhof ein
und vierzig Reichsthaler sieben Stüber zu bezahlen, und solche
laut Bericht in Rechnung zu bringen.

Mainz, den 4 May 1813. L. Glück.

Rf 41 „ 7 Stbr

PLATE 184: Heinrigs, Krefeld, 1813

Quittung.

Daß ich heute von Herrn Traugott Samuel Meyer Handelsmann in Rotterdam die mir seit voriger Oster-messe für verschiedene Waaren schuldig gebliebene eine Hundert Gulden empfangen habe, bescheinige ich hiermit.

Frankfurt, den 20 April 1813.

Jacob Zimmer.

PLATE 185: Heinrigs, Krefeld, 1813

a b c d e f g h i j k l m n o p

q r s ſ t u A B v w x y z

C D E F G H I K L M

N O P Q R S T U

V W X Y Z

Stirling scrip. *Girault sculp.*

PLATE 186: Stirling, Barcelona, 1830

Stirling scrip. *Girault sculp.*

PLATE 187: Stirling, Barcelona, 1830

ABCDEFGHIJK
LMNOPQRSTUVXYZ

PLATE 188: Stirling, Barcelona, 1830

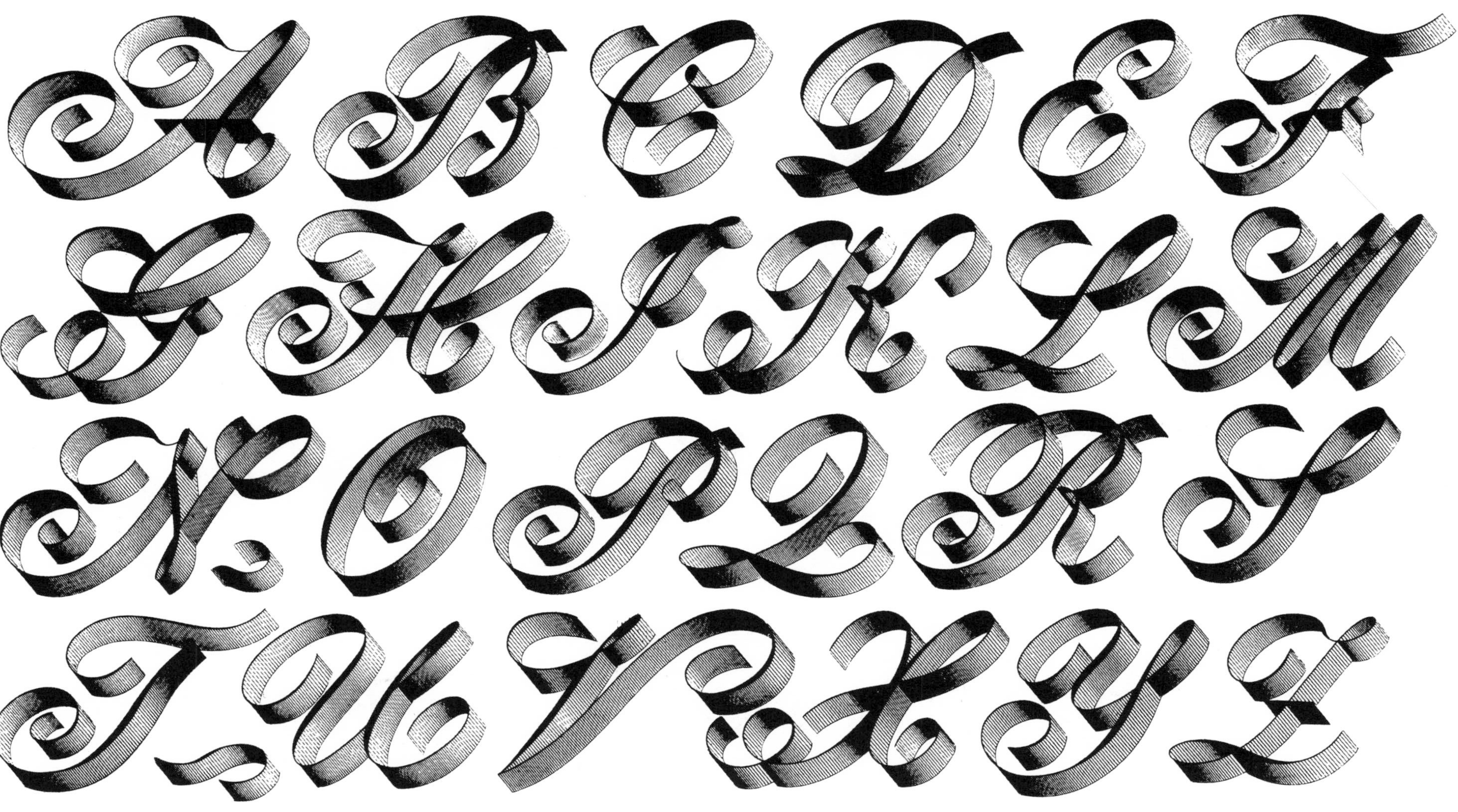

PLATE 189: Stirling, Barcelona, 1830

PLATE 190: Stirling, Barcelona, 1830

PLATE 191: Stirling, Barcelona, 1830

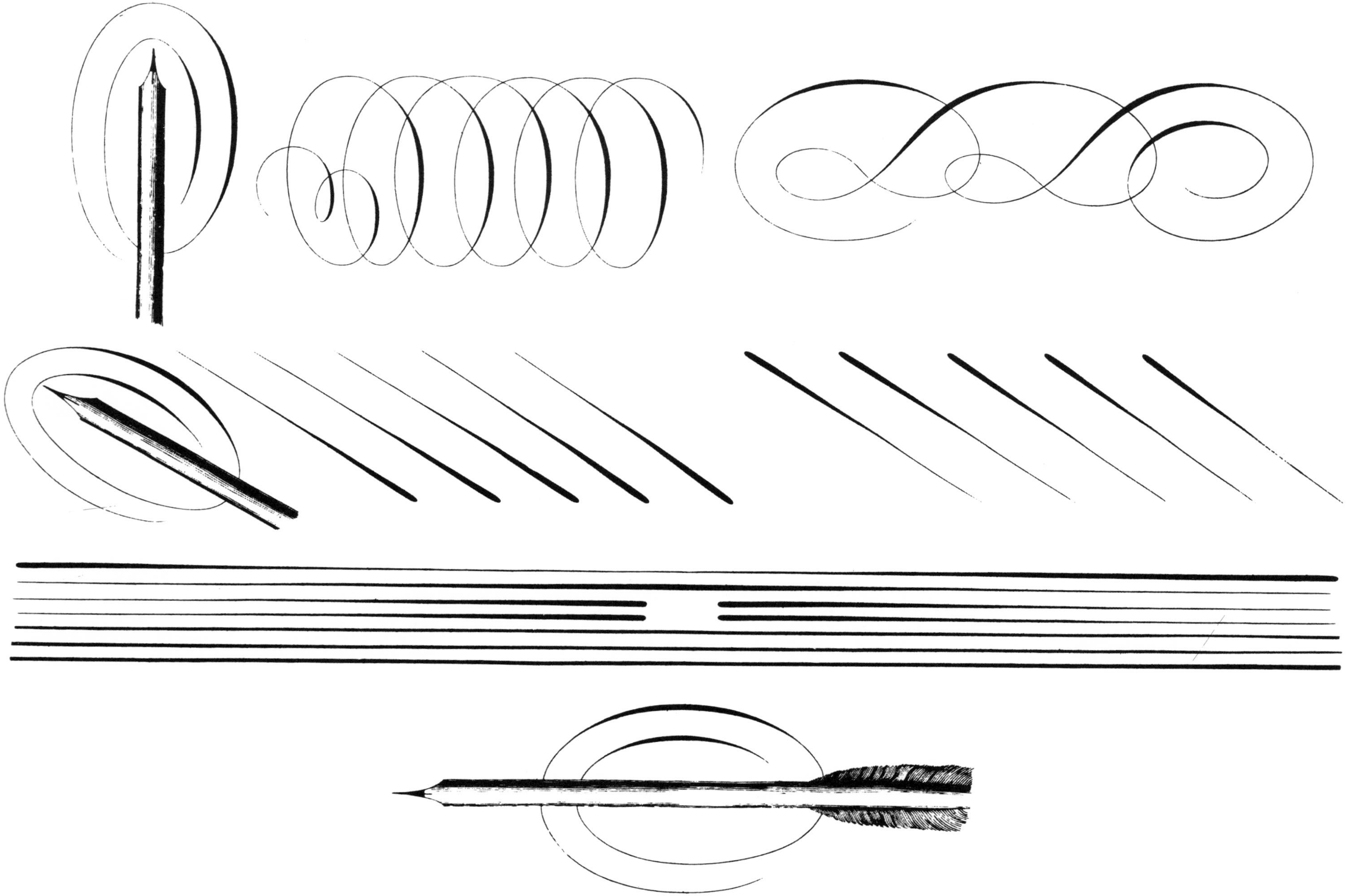

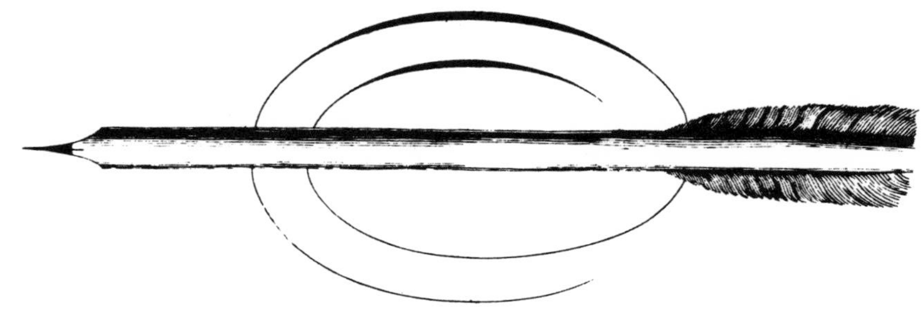

PLATE 192: Stirling, Barcelona, 1830

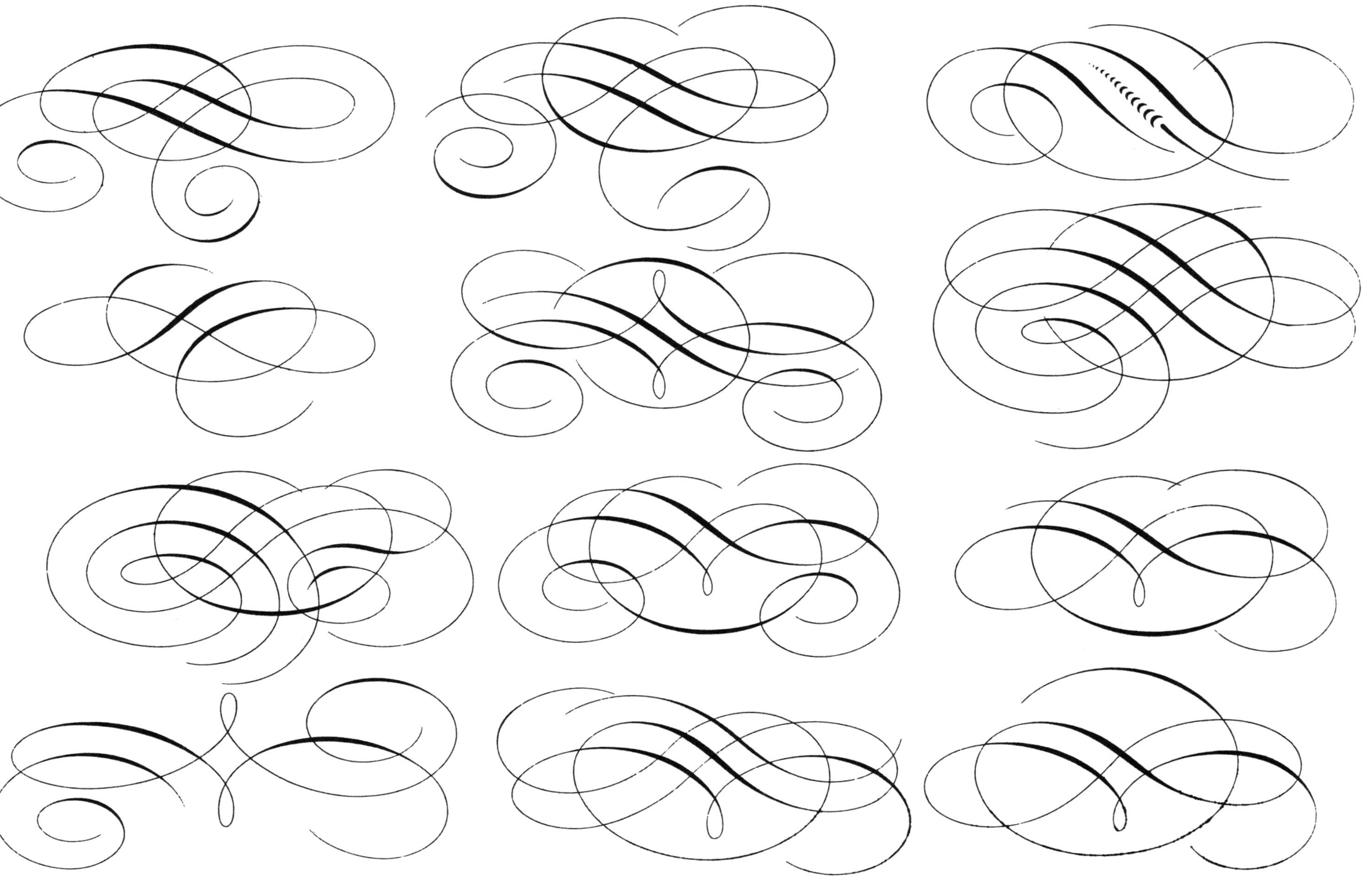

PLATE 193: Stirling, Barcelona, 1830

PLATE 194: Heinrigs, Cologne, 1831

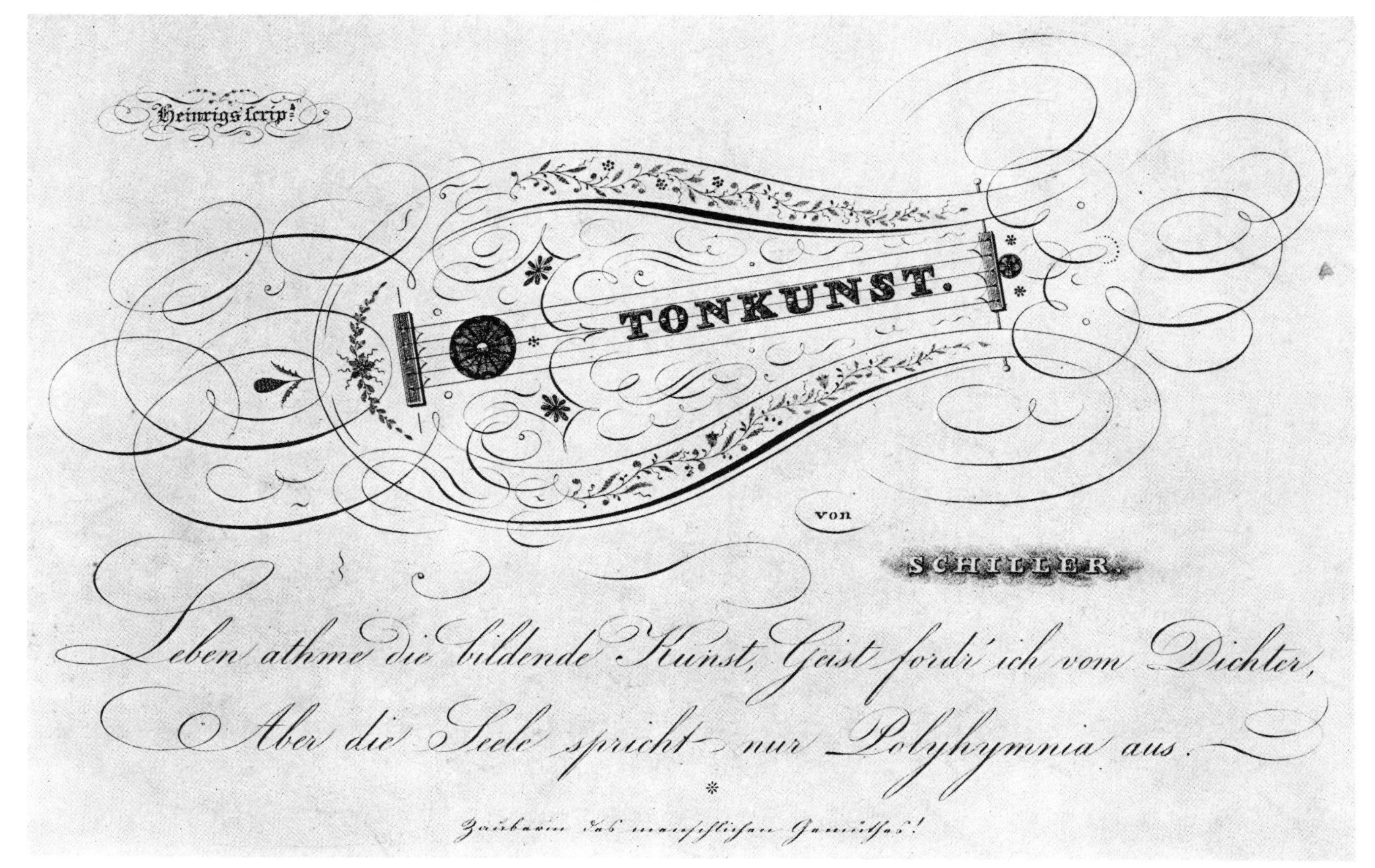

PLATE 195: Heinrigs, Cologne, 1831

Ecrit. mod. Pl. 15.

Alphabet Anglais à main levée

A B C D E F

G H I K L M

N O P Q R S T

U V W X Y Z

Midolle Ecrivain Composit.r Lith. d'E.d Simon Fils Edit.r à Strasbg.

PLATE 196: Midolle, Strasbourg, 1834–35

Ecrit. mod.

ALPHABET LAPIDAIRE MONSTRE.

Pl. 33.

ARNDT ARGENSON

BUFFON. BOSSUET

CICÉRON

DAGUESSEAU.

ESMENARD.

FLORIAN. FOY

GOETHE

HOLBEIN LA HARPE

IFFLAND

JACOBI

KOERNER KANT

LAHARPE. LEIBNITZ

Mozart MEIERBEER

Nicolai Newton

OBERLIN

PERRAULT

QUINAULT

RABELAIS Rossini

SCHILLER. SAUL

LE TASSE

UHLAND

VEGA

XIMENES XENOPHON

YOUNG. YRIARTE

ZSCHOKKE. ZEA

C. Fasoli

PLATE 197: Midolle, Strasbourg, 1834–35

PLATE 198: Midolle, Strasbourg, 1834–35

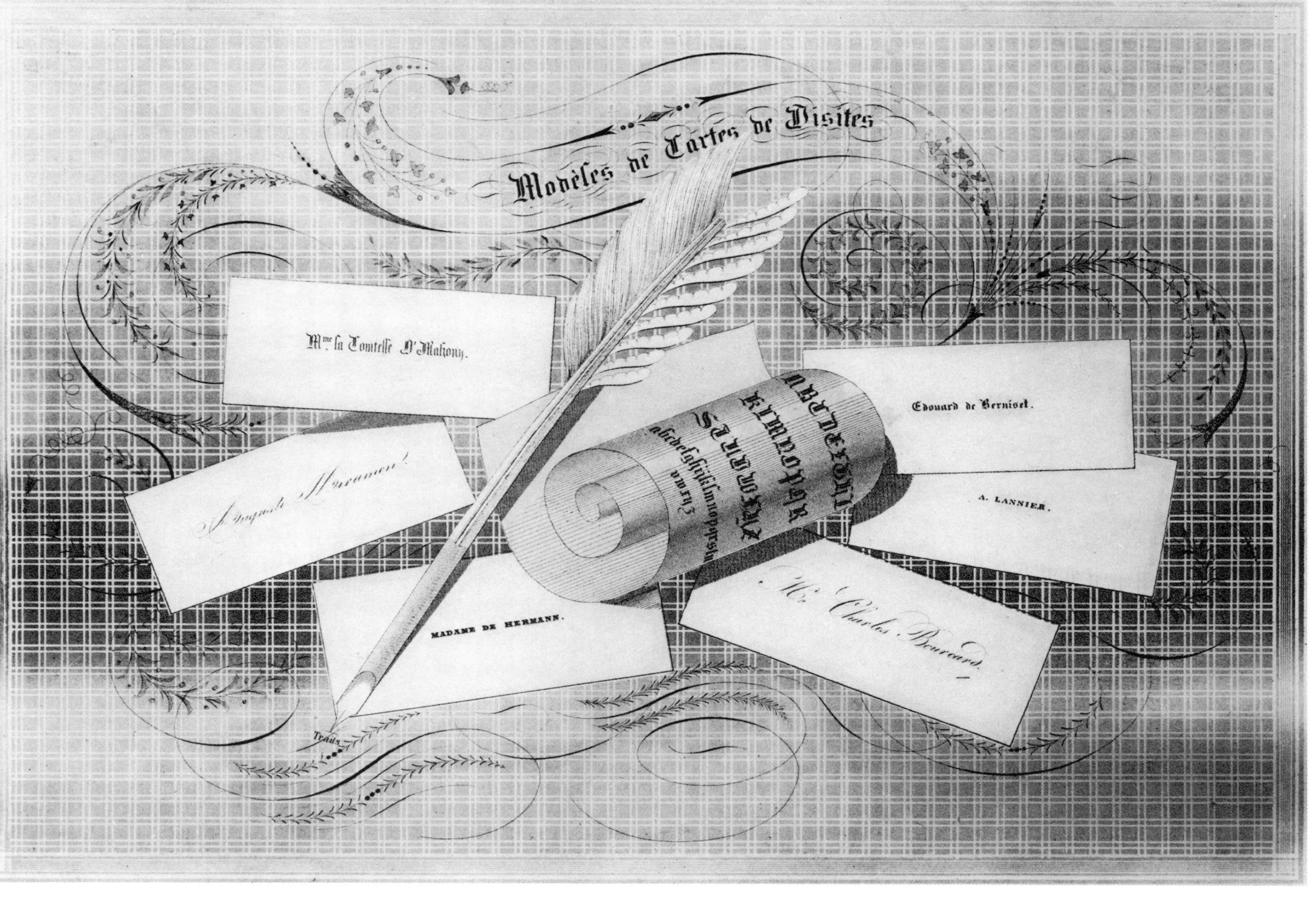

PLATE 199: Midolle, St. Gallen, 1840

PLATE 200: Petré, Paris, ca. 1670

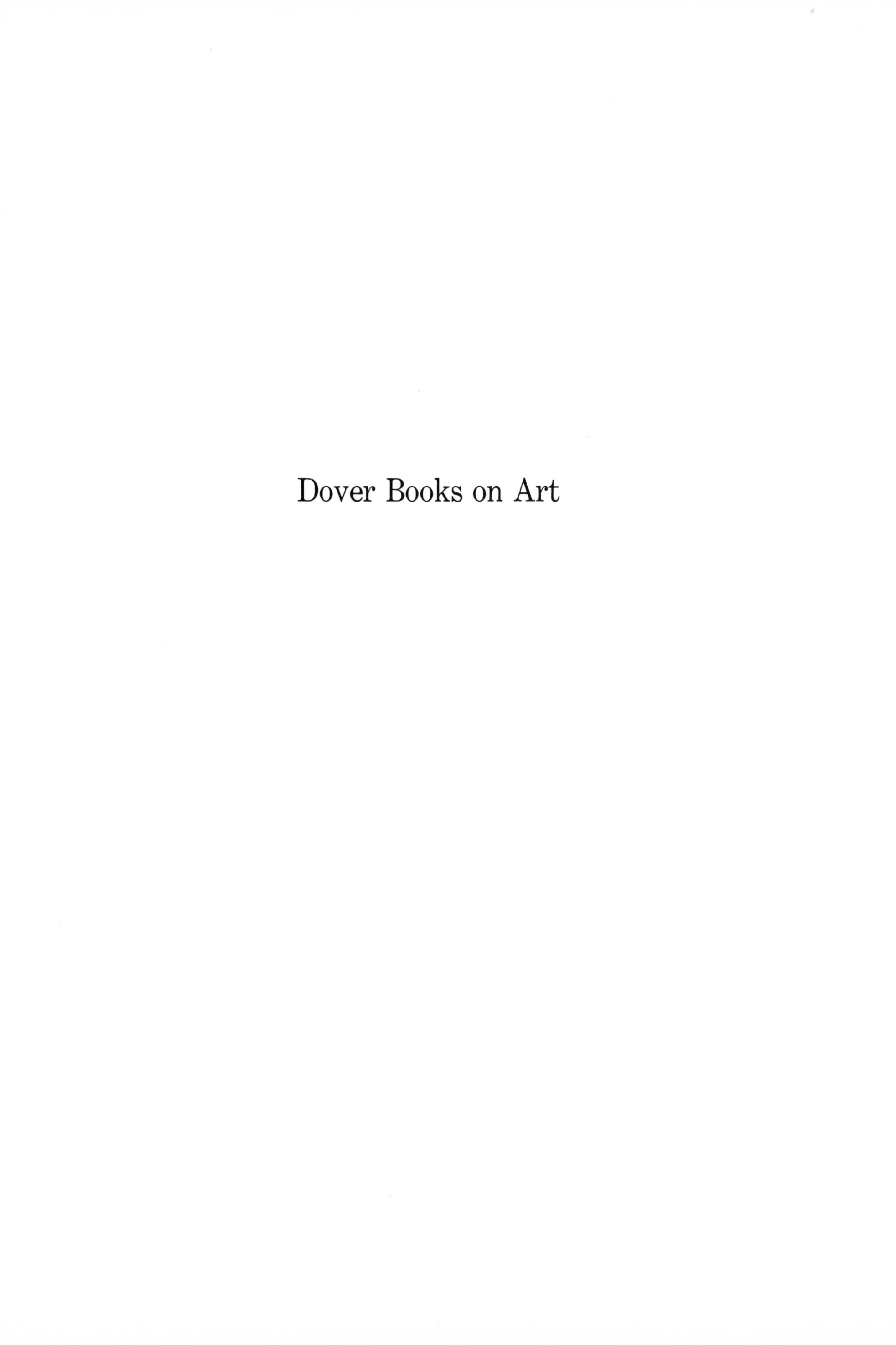

Dover Books on Art

Dover Books on Art

VITRUVIUS: TEN BOOKS ON ARCHITECTURE. The most influential book in the history of architecture. 1st century A.D. Roman classic has influenced such men as Bramante, Palladio, Michelangelo, up to present. Classic principles of design, harmony, etc. Fascinating reading. Definitive English translation by Professor H. Morgan, Harvard. 344pp. 5⅜ x 8.
20645-9 Paperbound **$5.00**

HAWTHORNE ON PAINTING. Vivid re-creation, from students' notes, of instructions by Charles Hawthorne at Cape Cod School of Art. Essays, epigrammatic comments on color, form, seeing, techniques, etc. "Excellent," Time. 100pp. 5⅜ x 8.
20653-X Paperbound **$2.25**

THE HANDBOOK OF PLANT AND FLORAL ORNAMENT, R. G. Hatton. 1200 line illustrations, from medieval, Renaissance herbals, of flowering or fruiting plants: garden flowers, wild flowers, medicinal plants, poisons, industrial plants, etc. A unique compilation that probably could not be matched in any library in the world. Formerly "The Craftsman's Plant-Book." Also full text on uses, history as ornament, etc. 548pp. 6⅛ x 9¼.
20649-1 Paperbound **$7.95**

DECORATIVE ALPHABETS AND INITIALS, Alexander Nesbitt. 91 complete alphabets, over 3900 ornamental initials, from Middle Ages, Renaissance printing, baroque, rococo, and modern sources. Individual items copyright free, for use in commercial art, crafts, design, packaging, etc. 123 full-page plates. 3924 initials. 129pp. 7¾ x 10¾. 20544-4 Paperbound **$6.00**

METHODS AND MATERIALS OF THE GREAT SCHOOLS AND MASTERS, Sir Charles Eastlake. (Formerly titled "Materials for a History of Oil Painting.") Vast, authentic reconstruction of secret techniques of the masters, recreated from ancient manuscripts, contemporary accounts, analysis of paintings, etc. Oils, fresco, tempera, varnishes, encaustics. Both Flemish and Italian schools, also British and French. One of great works for art historians, critics; inexhaustible mine of suggestions, information for practicing artists. Total of 1025pp. 5⅜ x 8.
20718-8, 20719-6 Two volume set, Paperbound **$15.00**

AMERICAN VICTORIAN ARCHITECTURE, edited by Arnold Lewis and Keith Morgan. Collection of brilliant photographs of 1870's, 1880's, showing finest domestic, public architecture; many buildings now gone. Landmark work, French in origin; first European appreciation of American work. Modern notes, introduction. 120 plates. "Architects and students of architecture will find this book invaluable for its first-hand depiction of the state of the art during a very formative period," ANTIQUE MONTHLY. 152pp. 9 x 12. 23177-1 Paperbound **$7.95**

THE HUMAN FIGURE, J. H. Vanderpoel. Not just a picture book, but a complete course by a famous figure artist. Extensive text, illustrated by 430 pencil and charcoal drawings of both male and female anatomy. 2nd enlarged edition. Foreword. 430 illus. 143pp. 6⅛ x 9¼. 20432-4 Paperbound **$3.50**

Dover Books on Art

PRINCIPLES OF ART HISTORY, H. Wölfflin. This remarkably instructive work demonstrates the tremendous change in artistic conception from the 14th to the 18th centuries, by analyzing 164 works by Botticelli, Dürer, Hobbema, Holbein, Hals, Titian, Rembrandt, Vermeer, etc., and pointing out exactly what is meant by "baroque," "classic," "primitive," "picturesque," and other basic terms of art history and criticism. "A remarkable lesson in the art of seeing," SAT. REV. OF LITERATURE. Translated from the 7th German edition. 150 illus. 254pp. 6⅛ x 9¼. 20276-3 Paperbound $4.95

FOUNDATIONS OF MODERN ART, A. Ozenfant. Stimulating discussion of human creativity from paleolithic cave painting to modern painting, architecture, decorative arts. Fully illustrated with works of Gris, Lipchitz, Léger, Picasso, primitive, modern artifacts, architecture, industrial art, much more. 226 illustrations. 368pp. 6⅛ x 9¼. 20215-1 Paperbound $6.95

METALWORK AND ENAMELLING, H. Maryon. Probably the best book ever written on the subject. Tells everything necessary for the home manufacture of jewelry, rings, ear pendants, bowls, etc. Covers materials, tools, soldering, filigree, setting stones, raising patterns, repoussé work, damascening, niello, cloisonné, polishing, assaying, casting, and dozens of other techniques. The best substitute for apprenticeship to a master metalworker. 363 photos and figures. 374pp. 5½ x 8½.
22702-2 Paperbound $5.00

SHAKER FURNITURE, E. D. and *F. Andrews.* The most illuminating study of Shaker furniture ever written. Covers chronology, craftsmanship, houses, shops, etc. Includes over 200 photographs of chairs, tables, clocks, beds, benches, etc. "Mr. & Mrs. Andrews know all there is to know about Shaker furniture," Mark Van Doren, NATION. 48 full-page plates. 192pp. 7⅞ x 10¾. 20679-3 Paperbound $5.00

LETTERING AND ALPHABETS, J. A. Cavanagh. An unabridged reissue of "Lettering," containing the full discussion, analysis, illustration of 89 basic hand lettering styles based on Caslon, Bodoni, Gothic, many other types. Hundreds of technical hints on construction, strokes, pens, brushes, etc. 89 alphabets, 72 lettered specimens, which may be reproduced permission-free. 121pp. 9¾ x 8. 20053-1 Paperbound $3.50

THE HUMAN FIGURE IN MOTION, Eadweard Muybridge. The largest collection in print of Muybridge's famous high-speed action photos. 4789 photographs in more than 500 action-strip-sequences (at shutter speeds up to 1/6000th of a second) illustrate men, women, children—mostly undraped—performing such actions as walking, running, getting up, lying down, carrying objects, throwing, etc. "An unparalleled dictionary of action for all artists," AMERICAN ARTIST. 390 full-page plates, with 4789 photographs. Heavy glossy stock, reinforced binding with headbands. 7⅞ x 10¾. 20204-6 Clothbound $15.95

Dover Books on Art

THE FOUR BOOKS OF ARCHITECTURE, Andrea Palladio. A compendium of the art of Andrea Palladio, one of the most celebrated architects of the Renaissance, including 250 magnificently-engraved plates showing edifices either of Palladio's design or reconstructed (in these drawings) by him from classical ruins and contemporary accounts. 257 plates. xxiv + 119pp. 9½ x 12¾. 21308-0 Paperbound $10.00

150 MASTERPIECES OF DRAWING, A. Toney. Selected by a gifted artist and teacher, these are some of the finest drawings produced by Western artists from the early 15th to the end of the 18th centuries. Excellent reproductions of drawings by Rembrandt, Bruegel, Raphael, Watteau, and other familiar masters, as well as works by lesser known but brilliant artists. 150 plates. xviii + 150pp. 5⅜ x 11¼. 21032-4 Paperbound $6.00

MORE DRAWINGS BY HEINRICH KLEY. Another collection of the graphic, vivid sketches of Heinrich Kley, one of the most diabolically talented cartoonists of our century. The sketches take in every aspect of human life: nothing is too sacred for him to ridicule, no one too eminent for him to satirize. 158 drawings you will not easily forget. iv + 104pp. 7⅜ x 10¾. 20041-8 Paperbound $3.75

STYLES IN PAINTING, Paul Zucker. By comparing paintings of similar subject matter, the author shows the characteristics of various painting styles. You are shown at a glance the differences between reclining nudes by Giorgione, Velasquez, Goya, Modigliani; how a Byzantine portrait is unlike a portrait by Van Eyck, da Vinci, Dürer, or Marc Chagall; how the painting of landscapes has changed gradually from ancient Pompeii to Lyonel Feininger in our own century. 241 beautiful, sharp photographs illustrate the text. xiv + 338 pp. 5⅝ x 8¼. 20760-9 Paperbound $6.50

PAINTING IN ISLAM, Sir Thomas W. Arnold. This scholarly study puts Islamic painting in its social and religious context and examines its relation to Islamic civilization in general. 65 full-page plates illustrate the text and give outstanding examples of Islamic art. 4 appendices. Index of mss. referred to. General Index. xxiv + 159pp. 6⅝ x 9¼. 21310-2 Paperbound $7.00

THE MATERIALS AND TECHNIQUES OF MEDIEVAL PAINTING, D. V. Thompson. An invaluable study of carriers and grounds, binding media, pigments, metals used in painting, al fresco and al secco techniques, burnishing, etc. used by the medieval masters. Preface by Bernard Berenson. 239pp. 5⅜ x 8. 20327-1 Paperbound $4.50

THE HISTORY AND TECHNIQUE OF LETTERING, A. Nesbitt. A thorough history of lettering from the ancient Egyptians to the present, and a 65-page course in lettering for artists. Every major development in lettering history is illustrated by a complete aphabet. Fully analyzes such masters as Caslon, Koch, Garamont, Jenson, and many more. 89 alphabets, 165 other specimens. 317pp. 7½ x 10½. 20427-8 Paperbound $5.50

Dover Books on Art

THE COMPLETE BOOK OF SILK SCREEN PRINTING PRODUCTION, J. I. Biegeleisen. Here is a clear and complete picture of every aspect of silk screen technique and press operation—from individually operated manual presses to modern automatic ones. Unsurpassed as a guidebook for setting up shop, making shop operation more efficient, finding out about latest methods and equipment; or as a textbook for use in teaching, studying, or learning all aspects of the profession. 124 figures. Index. Bibliography. List of Supply Sources. xi + 253pp. 5⅜ x 8½.
21100-2 Paperbound **$4.50**

A HISTORY OF COSTUME, Carl Köhler. The most reliable and authentic account of the development of dress from ancient times through the 19th century. Based on actual pieces of clothing that have survived, using paintings, statues and other reproductions only where originals no longer exist. Hundreds of illustrations, including detailed patterns for many articles. Highly useful for theatre and movie directors, fashion designers, illustrators, teachers. Edited and augmented by Emma von Sichart. Translated by Alexander K. Dallas. 594 illustrations. 464pp. 5⅛ x 7⅛.
21030-8 Paperbound **$6.50**

CHINESE HOUSEHOLD FURNITURE, G. N. Kates. A summary of virtually everything that is known about authentic Chinese furniture before it was contaminated by the influence of the West. The text covers history of styles, materials used, principles of design and craftsmanship, and furniture arrangement—all fully illustrated. xiii + 190pp. 5⅜ x 8½.
20958-X Paperbound **$4.00**

THE COMPLETE WOODCUTS OF ALBRECHT DURER, edited by Dr. Willi Kurth. Albrecht Dürer was a master in various media, but it was in woodcut design that his creative genius reached its highest expression. Here are all of his extant woodcuts, a collection of over 300 great works, many of which are not available elsewhere. An indispensable work for the art historian and critic and all art lovers. 346 plates. Index. 285pp. 8½ x 12¼. 21097-9 Paperbound $8.95

Dover publishes books on commercial art, art history, crafts, design, art classics; also books on music, literature, science, mathematics, puzzles and entertainments, chess, engineering, biology, philosophy, psychology, languages, history, and other fields. For free circulars write to Dept. DA, Dover Publications, Inc., 180 Varick St., New York, N.Y. 10014.